PERTH
TRAVEL

Hidden Gems, Insider Tips, & Budget-Friendly Adventures (full-color travel guide)

DANIEL C. FLICK

DANIEL C. FLICK

welcome to
PERTH

PERTH MAP

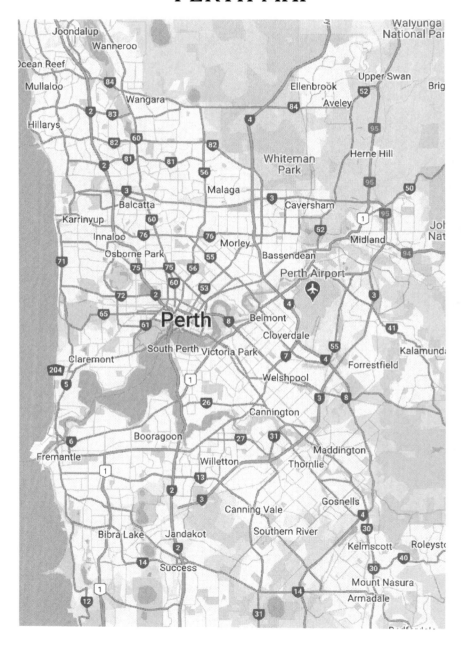

TABLE OF CONTENT

*PERTH MAP*_____4

*INTRODUCTION*_____9

  WHY VISIT PERTH_____12

  BEST TIME TO VISIT _____15

GETTING TO PERTH _____16

  ARRIVING BY AIR_____16

  ROAD TRIP AND SELF-DRIVING TO PERTH _____18

  TRAIN AND BUS TRAVEL OPTIONS _____21

*NAVIGATING THE CITY*_____25

  PUBLIC TRANSPORTATION IN PERTH _____25

  Other transportation options in Perth Coaches_____26

  TAXI AND RIDE-SHARING SERVICES_____27

  WALKING AND CYCLING AROUND PERTH _____28

TOP ATTRACTIONS IN PERTH _____31

  KINGS PARK AND BOTANIC GARDEN_____31

  Elizabeth Quay_____32

  PERTH ZOO _____33

  SWAN RIVER _____34

  THE TOWER BELL _____35

*EXPLORING PERTH'S BEACHES*_____38

  COTTESLOE BEACH _____38

CITY BEACH _____ 41

SCARBOROUGH BEACH _____ 42

BEST SURFING SPOTS_____ 43

CULTURAL AND HISTORICAL LANDMARKS _____ 46

PERTH CULTURAL CENTRE _____ 46

AUSTRALIA'S WESTERN ART GALLERY _____ 47

PRISON FREMANTLE_____ 49

THE PERTH MINT _____ 50

DAY TRIPS FROM PERTH _____ 52

ROTTNEST ISLAND_____ 52

SWAN VALLEY WINE REGION_____ 54

PINNACLES DESERT_____ 56

MARGARET RIVER REGION _____ 57

BEST OUTDOOR ACTIVITIES _____ 60

HIKING TRAILS AROUND PERTH _____ 60

CYCLING ROUTES_____ 61

WILDLIFE AND NATURE RESERVES IN PERTH_____ 63

RIVER CRUISES ON THE SWAN RIVER_____ 65

SHOPPING IN PERTH _____ 67

HAY STREET MALL AND MURRAY STREET MALL _____ 67

KING STREET: HIGH-END SHOPPING _____ 69

PERTH'S BEST MARKETS_____ 70

LOCAL SOUVENIRS TO BUY _____ 74

*WHERE TO EAT*_____ 78

LOCAL CUISINE _____ 78

TOP RESTAURANTS IN PERTH _____ 81

BEST CAFES AND BRUNCH SPOTS _____ 84

WHERE TO STAY IN PERTH _____ *88*

LUXURY HOTELS AND RESORTS _____ 88

BUDGET-FRIENDLY ACCOMMODATIONS _____ 90

FAMILY-FRIENDLY PLACES TO STAY _____ 92

NIGHTLIFE AND ENTERTAINMENT _____ *95*

PERTH'S BEST BARS AND PUBS _____ 95

LIVE MUSIC VENUES _____ 99

THEATRE AND PERFORMING ARTS _____ 100

TRAVEL TIPS AND SAFETY _____ *103*

STAYING SAFE IN PERTH _____ 103

HEALTH AND EMERGENCY CONTACTS _____ 104

LOCAL ETIQUETTE AND CUSTOMS _____ 105

CONCLUSION _____ *107*

INTRODUCTION

Stepping off the plane and feeling the warm, golden sunlight on my skin, I knew my trip to Perth was going to be something special. Perth isn't just another city – it's a place where the vibrancy of modern life meets the quiet serenity of untouched nature. From the moment I arrived, I felt like I was in a world where time flows a little slower, where the rhythm of life is set by the waves gently kissing the shore and the laughter of people enjoying life's simple pleasures.

Perth welcomed me with open arms. As I wandered its streets, I couldn't help but be drawn in by the city's charm – from the bustling energy of the Central Business District to the peaceful, laid-back vibe of its coastal neighborhoods. Every corner held a surprise, from trendy coffee spots tucked away in laneways to lively markets where locals come together in a celebration of food, art, and culture.

One afternoon, I found myself walking through Kings Park, an oasis of greenery with sweeping views of the city skyline and the Swan River. It was here, standing on the edge of this massive urban park, that I truly understood the beauty of Perth. It's a city that knows how to embrace both nature and progress. It's where you can take in panoramic views of a thriving metropolis one minute and lose yourself in the quiet tranquility of wildflowers and eucalyptus trees the next.

But what struck me was the people. Friendly, welcoming, and proud of their home, they were eager to share insider tips that would lead me to places off the beaten path – secluded beaches, hidden cafes, and cultural gems that many visitors might overlook. I remember sitting in a beachside restaurant, watching the sun dip below the horizon, painting the sky with shades of orange and pink, and feeling like I had discovered my little slice of paradise.

Perth, with its stunning landscapes, rich history, and vibrant culture, had become more than just a travel destination for me. It felt like a story that unfolded with every step I took, with every smile exchanged, with every sunset admired. And now, I'm here to share that story with you – to guide you through the wonders of this amazing city so that you, too, can experience the magic of Perth for yourself.

WHY VISIT PERTH

1. The seashores

Perth, which is regarded as the sunniest city in Australia, has more than 19 beaches that are easily accessible from the city. Every single one has unique qualities of its own. Each offers breathtakingly pure blue water and brilliant white beaches.

The most well-known is Cottesloe Beach, a well-liked location for picnics and swimming that is bordered by Norfolk pines, a verdant slope, and an incredibly gorgeous pavilion. You may swim, surf, or snorkel here for the whole day, and then go to a restaurant to watch the sunset over the Indian Ocean while sipping on the best Margaret River wine.

Leighton Beach, a longer, less crowded beach that's well-liked by dog owners and kite surfers, is located just south of Cottesloe. The ideal location to put on your snorkel is in Mettams Pool. Fish, octopuses, starfish, sea fans, and grasses may all be found on the platform reef that is located close offshore.

2. The fauna

It should come as no surprise that Perth is home to a wide variety of parks, natural reserves, and beaches. You can always expect to be "serenaded" by loud, colorful rosellas, galahs, and cockatoos as you wander through any metropolitan park.

The islands that surround Perth are also teeming with wildlife. Heirisson Island, a wildlife reserve with unrestricted access for kangaroos, is situated in the Swan River between Victoria Park and the East Perth suburbs. Together with dolphins and stingrays,

Penguin Island, located off the shore, is home to 1,200 juvenile penguins. You can get there via boat, and swimming with dolphins is a popular activity there.

Rottnest Island, which is a bit farther away, is the location of the greatest quokka population in the world. One of the prettiest creatures in the world and a bit of an Instagram sensation globally is the little, round-eyed, short-tailed wallaby. The best times to observe them are around dusk or late afternoon.

Volunteers who like working with animals may spend a day or two helping at Native Animal Rescue, located north of Perth. The organization takes in ill, wounded, and orphaned animals and tries to get them back into the wild.

3. The history of the Indigenous people
Perth is traditionally owned by the Noongar people, who hold the Swan River in high regard. They have several legends about the Wagyl, a water snake said to have created and maintained the majority of Perth's water features, including the river. It is reported that Wagyl formed the river by emerging from the earth at the base of Mount Eliza after entering the area close to Kings Park.

A fantastic way to start learning about the history of the city is with the Kings Park Indigenous Heritage Tour. Your guide will recount the Dreamtime account of the Noongar people's creation and discuss the cultural, medicinal, and nutritional significance of the nearby plants, animals, and landmarks. On the other hand, Indigenous Experiences Australia provides the two-hour Derbal

Yerrigan Cruise, a sailing excursion that explores the Whadjuk people's old culture along the Swan River.

4. The food and beverages

With new pubs, cafés, and restaurants sprouting up all the time, Perth has one of Australia's most active culinary scenes. Benefiting from Western Australia's sunny environment, it has the biggest number of rooftop pubs and outdoor dining establishments throughout the nation.

The seafood is incredible, which is not unexpected. The seafood on your dish will include barramundi from the north, lobster from Geraldton, oysters from Albany, prawns from Exmouth, scallops from neighboring Rottnest Island, and marron from the southwest of the state. Naturally, everything was paired with a Margaret River Sauvignon Blanc that won a prize.

If you like coffee, visit the well-known cappuccino strip in Fremantle. Beer enthusiasts could visit the Old Brewery, which is situated next to the Swan River, or the Little Creatures brewhouse, which has a view of Fremantle's harbor.

5. The Park of Kings

Kings Park, a 1,003-acre oasis of parks, botanical gardens, and natural bushland, is situated just on the western edge of Perth's central business area. It is larger and more untamed than Central Park in New York.

In addition to being home to over 324 native plant kinds, 215 recognized indigenous fungal species, and 80 bird species, the park provides expansive views of the CBD, Swan River, and Darling Range. One of the most recognizable structures in the city, the State War Memorial Cenotaph, may also be found here, along with playgrounds, a nature park, barbecue pits, and family picnic spots. Ascend the DNA Tower's spiral staircase for breathtaking views of Rottnest Island, the Swan River, Kings Park, and the Botanic Garden.

In addition, the park has an outdoor theater and hosts a range of events and performances.

BEST TIME TO VISIT

Perth is most enjoyable from March to May and from September to November. On the other hand, other individuals like the summertime heat to enjoy the beaches.

Amazing wildflowers may be seen from September to November, and the weather is mild with minimal rain.

The finest months for weather are March through May, when the sea is at its warmest and days are pleasant but nights are cold.

GETTING TO PERTH

ARRIVING BY AIR

Arriving by Air: Perth Airport Guide

Landing in Perth is an experience in itself, as you catch a glimpse of the sprawling city nestled between the Swan River and the Indian Ocean. Perth Airport, your gateway to Western Australia, is modern, efficient, and well-equipped to ensure a smooth arrival for both domestic and international travelers.

Terminals and Layout

Perth Airport consists of four main terminals, divided between two precincts: T1/T2 and T3/T4. Terminal 1 handles most international flights and some domestic routes, while Terminal 2 caters to regional flights. Terminals 3 and 4, located in a separate precinct, manage the bulk of domestic flights for Qantas and Virgin Australia. Shuttle services run between the two precincts, ensuring easy transfers if your journey requires switching terminals.

International Arrivals

If you're arriving internationally, Terminal 1 is where your Perth adventure begins. The immigration process is usually quick and straightforward, with friendly staff ready to assist if needed. The airport features automated SmartGates, making entry even smoother for eligible passport holders. After clearing customs, you'll find baggage claim nearby, followed by quarantine screening, a standard procedure in Australia to protect the country's unique ecosystem.

Domestic Arrivals

For domestic travelers, Terminals 3 and 4 are easily navigable, with clear signage leading you from the gate to baggage claim. After collecting your luggage, you'll be able to head directly out to ground transportation, where taxis, ride-sharing services, and shuttle buses are readily available.

Transport Options

One of the most convenient aspects of Perth Airport is the variety of transport options. If you're looking for a hassle-free journey to the city center, taxis and ride-sharing services like Uber and Ola are available directly outside the arrivals area. A trip to the city takes about 20 minutes, depending on traffic.

For a more economical option, the Airport Central Bus Station connects the airport to Perth's public transport system via Bus Route 380, offering a reliable service to the city and surrounding suburbs. The buses run frequently, and fares are affordable, making this a great choice for budget-conscious travelers.

Car Rentals and Parking

If you prefer the flexibility of driving, Perth Airport offers several car rental companies, including Avis, Budget, and Hertz. Rental counters are located near the baggage claim areas, making it easy to pick up your car and head off on your adventure. There are also ample parking options at the airport, including short-term and long-term lots, perfect for travelers with varying needs.

Airport Facilities

Perth Airport offers a range of amenities to ensure your arrival or departure is as comfortable as possible. There are plenty of dining options, from quick bites at fast-food outlets to sit-down meals at cafes and restaurants. Free Wi-Fi is available throughout the terminals, allowing you to stay connected. You'll also find duty-free shopping, ATMs, currency exchange services, and information desks where you can get help if needed.

ROAD TRIP AND SELF-DRIVING TO PERTH

For those with a love for open roads and scenic adventures, driving to Perth is a road trip like no other. Whether you're arriving from another part of Western Australia or embarking on the cross-country journey from the East Coast, self-driving to Perth promises unforgettable landscapes and a sense of freedom that only a long road trip can deliver.

The Great Australian Road Trip
Driving to Perth from the eastern states of Australia is not for the faint-hearted, but for true road-trip enthusiasts, it's an epic adventure. The journey typically involves traveling across the iconic Nullarbor Plain, a vast, arid expanse that stretches over 1,200 kilometers, offering some of the most remote and desolate landscapes in the country. While the drive requires careful planning, the experience is rewarding, providing stunning views of the Outback, a chance to see wildlife like kangaroos and emus, and the remarkable feeling of isolation in one of the world's most uninhabited areas.

Suggested Routes

- From Adelaide to Perth: This route, around 2,700 kilometers, is one of the most popular for those embarking on the transcontinental road trip. It takes you through the Nullarbor, across Eyre Highway, and past attractions like the Head of Bight, where you can stop to watch migrating whales during certain seasons. With plenty of roadside stops and roadhouses, this route is adventurous but manageable for most travelers.

- From Melbourne to Perth: This longer drive, spanning about 3,400 kilometers, offers a mix of city, coast, and desert. The route generally follows the same path as the Adelaide-Perth drive once you reach South Australia, but with an added section along the scenic Great Ocean Road before heading into the vastness of the Outback.

- From the North (Broome to Perth): If you're exploring Western Australia, the drive from Broome to Perth is another incredible option. Covering around 2,200 kilometers, this road trip takes you through the wild and rugged Kimberley region, the stunning gorges of Karijini National Park, and the stunning coastline along Ningaloo Reef. It's an ideal route for those who want to experience Western Australia's diverse landscapes, from red deserts to pristine beaches.

What to Expect on the Road
Self-driving to Perth is not just about getting from point A to point B—it's about the journey itself. Western Australia is vast, and you'll pass through long stretches of untouched wilderness, coastal roads, and charming outback towns. One of the joys of road-tripping to Perth is the ever-changing scenery, from the wild

coastal cliffs of the Great Australian Bight to the rolling dunes of the Wheatbelt region.

While the roads are generally well-maintained, the sheer distance between stops, especially in the more remote areas, means preparation is key. Fuel stops can be hundreds of kilometers apart, so carrying extra fuel and water is essential. Rest areas and roadhouses offer basic services, but it's important to stock up on supplies and ensure your vehicle is in top condition before embarking on the journey.

Exploring Perth by Car
Once you arrive in Perth, having your vehicle opens up even more opportunities for exploration. The city itself is easy to navigate, with wide streets, clear signage, and plenty of parking options. Driving gives you the flexibility to venture out to nearby attractions like the beaches of Cottesloe and Scarborough, the wineries of the Swan Valley, or even farther afield to destinations like Margaret River or the Pinnacles Desert.

Safety Tips for Long-Distance Driving
- Plan your stops: Break up the long journey with overnight stays at roadhouses or motels. Not only will this give you a chance to rest, but it also allows you to explore more of the smaller towns and sights along the way.

- Stay alert: Fatigue can be a major risk on such long drives. Share the driving if possible, and take regular breaks. Australia's outback roads can be straight and monotonous, making it easy to lose focus.

- Watch for wildlife: Kangaroos and other animals are more active at dawn and dusk, so it's best to avoid driving during these times, particularly in remote areas.

TRAIN AND BUS TRAVEL OPTIONS

Traveling to Perth by train or bus offers a unique and scenic way to experience Australia's vast landscapes, whether you're journeying from the eastern states or exploring within Western Australia. While air travel might be faster, these modes of transport provide a slower, more immersive way to take in the country's natural beauty, with a mix of comfort, affordability, and adventure.

Train Travel: The Indian Pacific
One of the most iconic train journeys in Australia, and indeed the world, is the Indian Pacific, which runs between Sydney and Perth. Covering over 4,000 kilometers, this legendary train ride allows you to travel from coast to coast, crossing the vast expanse of the Nullarbor Plain and experiencing the sheer size and diversity of Australia's landscapes.

What to Expect
The Indian Pacific offers a truly luxurious experience for train enthusiasts. It's not just a means of transport; it's a journey of a lifetime. The trip takes approximately 65 hours, with multiple stops along the way, including Adelaide and Kalgoorlie. You'll have the chance to step off the train at select points to explore local sights, such as Adelaide's vibrant food scene or the gold mining town of Kalgoorlie.

Onboard, the Indian Pacific provides different classes of service, from Gold and Platinum class with private cabins and gourmet dining, to the more economical Red Service, offering reclining seats for budget-conscious travelers. Meals and drinks are often included in the fare, with dining cars serving high-quality food inspired by regional Australian cuisine.

The highlight of the journey is undoubtedly the breathtaking scenery, which ranges from the Blue Mountains' lush greenery to the stark, endless plains of the outback. It's a once-in-a-lifetime experience for those who enjoy slow travel and appreciate the charm of railway adventures.

Bus Travel: Affordable and Scenic
If you're looking for a more budget-friendly way to travel to Perth, long-distance buses provide an affordable and scenic option. Australia's national bus companies, like **Greyhound Australia** and **Integrity Coach Lines**, offer regular services to and from Perth, connecting it with cities such as Adelaide, Darwin, and Broome.

Bus Routes to Perth
- From Adelaide to Perth: This route is approximately 2,700 kilometers and takes about 36 hours. The journey passes through some incredible landscapes, including the Eyre Peninsula, Nullarbor Plain, and Southern Ocean coastline. While the trip is long, the bus makes regular stops for food and rest, allowing passengers to stretch their legs and take in the surroundings.

- From Broome to Perth: For those exploring Western Australia, Integrity Coach Lines offers a popular route between Broome and

Perth, covering 2,200 kilometers over 24 hours. The route takes you through the scenic coastal and inland areas of Western Australia, with stops at places like Karratha and Carnarvon along the way.

- Regional and Local Bus Travel: Western Australia also has a reliable network of regional buses that connect Perth with nearby towns and attractions, such as Margaret River, Albany, and the Pinnacles Desert. These shorter routes provide a convenient option for travelers looking to explore beyond Perth without renting a car.

What to Expect
Bus travel offers a comfortable, if longer, journey across Australia. Most long-distance buses are equipped with reclining seats, air conditioning, onboard toilets, and Wi-Fi. Greyhound and Integrity Coach Lines also offer flexible tickets, allowing passengers to hop on and off at various points along their route, making it easier to explore more remote areas of the country.

Bus journeys to Perth can be an affordable option for travelers who don't mind a longer trip. With several stops along the way, it's also a great opportunity to take in Australia's vast, changing landscapes at a slower pace, from the rugged coastline to the open plains of the outback.

Practical Tips for Train and Bus Travel
- Booking in Advance: Whether you're taking the Indian Pacific or a long-distance bus, it's best to book your tickets in advance, especially during peak travel seasons. Train journeys, in

particular, can fill up quickly, as they are a popular tourist attraction.

- Prepare for Long Journeys: Both train and bus travel to Perth involves long hours on the road or tracks, so it's essential to pack snacks, entertainment, and any personal comforts you might need for the journey. While food is available onboard trains and buses, having your supplies can make the trip more enjoyable.

- Embrace the Scenic Views: The journey is as much a part of the adventure as the destination. Whether it's the stunning outback sunsets from your train window or the expansive coastline from your bus seat, take the time to enjoy the unique landscapes Australia has to offer.

NAVIGATING THE CITY

PUBLIC TRANSPORTATION IN PERTH

Perth's excellent weather makes walking and bicycling year-round, and public transportation makes getting about the city simple. Here's how to navigate Perth easily.

Perth's Public Transportation
Perth has a comprehensive bus, rail, and ferry public transportation network. It is advised that you get a Transperth SmartRider card to use the network. SmartRider retail stores, Transperth InfoCentres, and Perth Airport all sell SmartRider cards. You may get a daily spending cap and a fare reduction with your SmartRider card.

Before using Perth's public transportation alternatives, you must load funds onto your SmartRider card to pay for your fares.
When you board the vehicle of your choice and make sure to touch again when you get off, your ride will begin. Simply tap your card on the scanner.

Using public transportation to get to Perth
The train system in Perth is an excellent means of getting to the neighboring suburbs and
downtown attractions. Trains connecting City West, Elizabeth Quay, and Claisebrook stations may run through a free transit zone located in the city center. You must tap on and off using a SmartRider card to benefit from the free fares.

Driving in and out of Perth

While driving in Perth is simple and safe, you may find that using a mix of public transportation, ridesharing, and taxis is a more convenient way to travel about the city.

If you decide to hire a vehicle in the city or at the airport, you may wish to find out whether your hotel has daily parking fees.

Throughout the city, the City of Perth manages a large number of off-street parking lots.

Other transportation options in Perth Coaches

Another excellent method to experience Perth's sites is on the hop-on, hop-off Perth Explorer bus. One-day or two-day tickets are available for purchase.

Ferries

Regular electric private ferry services connecting Elizabeth Quay, the On the Point entertainment and eating district, and Optus Stadium are provided by The Little Ferry Co. along the Swan River.

The Rottnest Express and SeaLink ferries are two more private ferry services that may take you from Perth to Rottnest Island.

Cruises

Taking a ride on the Swan River, a stunning canal that winds through the heart of Perth is a fantastic way to view the city.

Captain Cook Excursions offers lengthier trips to the adjacent port city of Fremantle, in addition to picturesque Swan River excursions.

Daily Swan River trips and cruises to Carnac Island, off Fremantle, are provided by Wild West Charters.

TAXI AND RIDE-SHARING SERVICES

Getting around Perth is a breeze, thanks to the availability of taxis and ride-sharing services that cater to travelers looking for convenience and flexibility.

Taxis

Perth's taxi services are reliable, widely available, and easy to use. Taxis can be hailed on the street, found at designated taxi ranks throughout the city, or booked in advance through apps or by phone. Major taxi companies like Swan Taxis and Black & White Cabs offer 24/7 services, ensuring that you can always find a ride, even late at night or during peak hours.

Fares are metered and start with a base charge, with additional costs based on the distance traveled and any waiting time. While taxis are generally more expensive than public transport, they offer door-to-door service, making them ideal for those with luggage, mobility needs, or tight schedules. Drivers are required to adhere to strict service standards, so you can expect a clean, safe, and comfortable ride.

Ride-Sharing Services

For a more affordable and tech-savvy option, ride-sharing services like Uber and Ola are widely used in Perth. These apps allow you to book a ride directly from your smartphone, track your driver's location, and get an upfront price estimate before you even get in the car. Ride-sharing is often quicker and cheaper than taxis, especially for short trips around the city.

Both Uber and Ola operate in Perth's city center, suburbs, and beyond, offering a range of ride options, from budget-friendly services to more luxurious rides. The cashless payment system makes it convenient for travelers, and with frequent promotions and discounts available, ride-sharing can be a cost-effective way to get around Perth.

WALKING AND CYCLING AROUND PERTH

One of the most enjoyable ways to explore Perth is on foot or by bike. The city's compact layout, combined with its mild climate and abundant parks, makes walking and cycling a pleasant and accessible option for visitors. Whether you're strolling through the heart of the city or cycling along the picturesque Swan River, you'll find that Perth's urban design encourages active exploration.

Walking Around Perth
Perth is a highly walkable city, with many of its top attractions located within proximity to one another. The city's streets are well-maintained, with wide, pedestrian-friendly footpaths, plenty of green spaces, and a network of walking trails that make it easy to discover hidden gems. Whether you're browsing the shops along Hay Street, taking in the views from Kings Park, or wandering through the vibrant Northbridge district, walking is a

great way to immerse yourself in the city's culture and atmosphere.

The central business district (CBD) is relatively flat, making it accessible for people of all ages and fitness levels. Perth also offers a variety of free walking tours that provide insight into the city's history, art, and local culture. If you prefer exploring at your own pace, maps and guidebooks are available to help you navigate the city's key sights and neighborhoods.

Cycling in Perth
Perth is increasingly becoming a cycling-friendly city, with an extensive network of dedicated bike lanes and shared paths that make getting around on two wheels both safe and enjoyable. Whether you're a casual rider or an experienced cyclist, you'll find routes to suit all levels, from leisurely rides along the river to more challenging trails that take you out to the coast or through the city's surrounding parks.

One of the most popular cycling routes in Perth is the Swan River Loop, which offers stunning views of the river, city skyline, and nearby neighborhoods. This 10-kilometer loop is a favorite for locals and visitors alike, providing a scenic and relaxing ride with plenty of spots to stop and take in the sights.

For those without their bikes, Perth's bike-sharing scheme, Spinway, offers a convenient way to rent bikes from several stations around the city. Bike rentals are affordable, and with Perth's excellent weather, it's a great way to spend a day exploring the city. Alternatively, many hotels and local bike shops offer bike rentals, making it easy for visitors to enjoy Perth's cycling paths.

TOP ATTRACTIONS IN PERTH

KINGS PARK AND BOTANIC GARDEN

Kings Park and Botanic Garden, one of the biggest inner-city parks in the world, is 400 hectares of calm, natural bushland and beautifully designed gardens situated in the center of Perth. Located on Mount Eliza's crest, it's an ideal location for seeing expansive vistas of Perth's urban landscape and Swan River.

Take a free CAT bus or walk 15 minutes from Perth's city center to Kings Park with a picnic or grill. Get free walking tours, self-guided tours, and maps and brochures at the visitor information center.

Come have coffee with the locals at one of the cafés, or have lunch and supper at the upscale eatery. While the kids play on the playgrounds, unwind. Explore the Lotterywest Federation Walkway's treetops while learning about the region's wildlife, Indigenous culture, and European history.

The State War Memorial and State Botanic Garden are located in Kings Park, which was the first public park in Australia to be declared open to the public in 1872. It has 1,700 distinct native species and a spectacular springtime wildflower display, which is commemorated with the September Kings Park Festival.

Facilities: Picnic area, public phone, public restroom, restaurant, barbecue, cafe, car park, coach parking, conference/convention facilities, interactive center, kiosk, pet-friendly - inquire

Free admission Location
West Perth, Australia's Fraser Avenue 6005

Elizabeth Quay

On the banks of the Swan River is a brand-new, vibrant waterfront district called Elizabeth Quay.

In Perth, the place to be seen and seen. The BHP Billiton Water Park, the island playground, promenades, open areas, and a variety of eateries and cafes can all be found here.

Accessible by public transportation, the Transperth Ferry terminal is situated in the inlet, the free blue CAT bus stops next to the Bell Tower, and the Elizabeth Quay Train and Bus Port is only a short walk away.

Visitors and residents may take a variety of picturesque river excursions from Barrack Street Jetty to the Swan Valley, Fremantle, and Rottnest Island.

There are many other things to do in the region, including taking a leisurely walk along the river, pausing for a selfie on the bridge, riding the gondola on the Swan, or using a Segway. Additionally, twenty-four short-term public boat moorings are offered.

Because of its outstanding waterfront position, Elizabeth Quay is a year-round destination for events and entertainment.

Location: Perth, WA 6000, The Esplanade

Email address (08) 9482 7499

PERTH ZOO

Located in South Perth, the Perth Zoo is just five minutes from the city center and is home to animals and plants from all over the globe.

See kangaroos, emus, koalas, quokkas, and Simmo the big crocodile by going on a bushwalk. See Sumatran tigers, Asian elephants, gibbons, and sun bears up close as you explore the Asian Rainforest. Meet lions, giraffes, zebras, rhinos, and meerkats as you explore the African Savannah. These and more animals from throughout the globe may be found in Perth Zoo.

Start a full day of talks about free keepers. If you're courageous, you could book an Eye to Eye session, which allows you to interact closely with creatures like bearded dragons, giraffes, and quokkas.

For young toddlers and families, the Perth Zoo is an excellent choice. Children under four enter free of charge, while families and groups get reduced fees.

A membership to Zoo Friends is quite inexpensive and offers a ton of other amazing benefits, including annual unrestricted access to the zoo. 10% of membership fees are waived for City of South Perth residents.
Check the zoo's website before you visit since they often organize special events.

The Perth Zoo and the City of South Perth

The history and expansion of Perth Zoo are closely linked to those of the City of South Perth.

Perth Zoo was established in 1898 and became a popular leisure destination in the early years of colonial settlement.

Perth Zoo's attraction to tourists from all over the world, as well as West Australians, has led to an expansion of the region's transportation linkages and infrastructure, notably its ferry services.

Perth Zoo is a popular destination and a part of the global conservation community. It is a state-of-the-art zoo that provides generations of Western Australians and their families with memorable experiences. The goals of the zoo are to promote an appreciation of biodiversity, strengthen linkages between people and the natural world, and provide individuals with practical chances to make significant contributions to animal conservation.

What unites the City of South Perth with the Perth Zoo is a shared commitment to sustainability, education, the environment, and community.

08 9474 0444 is the phone number for Perth Zoo. OPTIONS: 9 a.m. to 5 p.m., Monday through Friday. ADDRESS Twenty Labouchere Road, South Perth

SWAN RIVER

Enjoy one of the most picturesque cityscapes from the Swan River and its shoreline, and join the people of Perth for a stroll, a jog, a cycling, a picnic, a sailing and fishing excursion, or a leisurely river cruise. With Perth's magnificent blue sky and several vantage points providing ideal shooting possibilities, the city stands proudly on its banks. For an expansive 180-degree view of the river, the town, and the Darling Range beyond, visit Kings Park and Botanic Garden.

Take a leisurely lunch on the South Perth boat or unwind on Matilda Bay's expansive beach.

Traverse the river towards Fremantle, where you may see some of Perth's most lavish riverfront homes. Alternatively, take a trip to the higher reaches to experience the bounty and history of the Swan Valley, the oldest wine area in Western Australia.

For those seeking excitement on the ocean, consider renting a surf cat, going twilight sailing, getting on a jet ski, or throwing in a fishing line.

The Avon Descent, a demanding two-day time trial that pits amateurs and Olympic winners from all over the world against each other, takes place in the Swan River during the winter. Arrange a spot by the riverside to see this breathtaking show.

Facilities include a picnic area, public restrooms, restaurants, shops, gift shops, barbecues, cafes, car parks, coach parking, and pet-friendly accommodations.

THE TOWER BELL

Perth City is filled with the sound of one of the biggest musical instruments in the world, chiming from the top of the Bell Tower's soaring glass spire. The bells are the original bells of St. Martin-in-the-Fields Church, the parish church of Buckingham Palace located in London's Trafalgar Square, dating back to the fourteenth century.

It's one of the few locations on Earth where guests can see the age-old craft of bell ringing in action and even try their hand at ringing the bells thanks to interactive demonstrations.

The ANZAC Bell was just erected in the Bell Tower in addition to the St. Martin bells. Cast in Perth, it's the biggest bell of its sort ever manufactured in Australia. The ANZAC Bell weighs 6,500 kg and is predicted to survive for more than 500 years.

Impressive insights into the history of the bells and bell ringing are shared via the informative exhibits. Situated on the sixth level, the outdoor observation deck offers breathtaking views of the city and Swan River.

One of Perth's most popular must-see sights, this award-winning venue is situated in Barrack Square, where the City meets the Swan River, and is just a five-minute walk from the City Center.

Facilities include a family-friendly gallery or museum, an interactive center, lookouts, a public restroom, a shop or gift shop, and an information desk.

Opening Hours
Thursday: 10 a.m.–4 p.m.
Friday: 10 a.m. to 4 p.m.
Saul: 10 a.m.–4 p.m.
Sunday: 10 a.m. to 4 p.m.
Tuesday from 10 a.m. to 4 p.m.
Wednesday, 10 a.m.–4 p.m.
Monday: Not open
Christmas Day: Not Open
March 29: Not Open

Admission price
Each ticket is $10–$66.
Children: $22 - free

Location: Riverside Drive and Barrack Square, Perth, Western Australia, 6000

Call (618) 6210-0444 or (618) 6210-0402

EXPLORING PERTH'S BEACHES

COTTESLOE BEACH

The famous Cottesloe Beach in Perth is breathtaking. It's a well-liked location for swimming, snorkeling, surfing, and enjoying a glass of wine, a crisp beer, or a leisurely supper while watching the sunset over the ocean.

From Perth, 'Cott,' as it's lovingly called, is accessible by car, bus, or rail. Walk the 600 metres to the beach from Cottesloe station, or take the frequent Transperth buses, a 15-minute drive from the city, or the Fremantle rail line.

Its many attractions are what make it a favorite among Perth's nineteen breathtaking white sand beaches. The ideal environment for a leisurely day or family outing is provided by the serene beaches, silky terraced lawns, and shaded Norfolk pines.

Enjoy breakfast, lunch, supper, sunset cocktails, or a boisterous Sunday session by the beach at this bustling promenade of eateries, cafés, and bars.

Swimmers, bodyboarders, and surfers frequent the area because of the crystal-clear seas and steady waves, while snorkelers are encouraged to enter the ocean by the nearby rocks and reefs.

Additionally, in March, Sculpture by the Sea will turn the waterfront into the most amazing outdoor exhibition.

One of Perth's treasures for a long time has been Cottesloe Beach, or "Cott" as the locals refer to it. Stretching over a kilometer (0.6 km) down the shore, its pristine white sand meets incredibly blue water that is loved for swimming, surfing, and snorkeling. Unwind under the shade of the Norfolk Pines, go snorkeling around a vibrant coral, and have dinner with a view of the Indian Ocean. The best activities in Cottesloe Beach are listed here.

See the Sculpture by the Sea exhibit.
Reopening in March is the yearly Sculpture by the Sea, a free waterfront art exhibition with massive and intriguing sculptures that border Cottesloe Beach. See interesting works by established and emerging artists as you go down the coast and across the grassy area towards North Cottesloe.

Take in the Indian Ocean vistas while dining.
Cottesloe's stylish beachside eateries provide unrivalled dining views and cuisines to match. Take a seat at Longview for contemporary Australian cuisine served from dawn to sundown with stunning views, or at Barchetta to enjoy fresh Mediterranean food while admiring the blue Indian Ocean.

Go swimming and snorkeling. Ocean lovers are lured to Cottesloe's colorful reefs and pristine waters all year round. If it's a calm day, go to South Cottesloe to look for the critically endangered leafy sea dragon. Alternatively, bring your snorkel to the protected Peters Pool at North Cottesloe Beach. Stay in the area between the yellow and red beach flags if you can swim.

Surf the surf.

Not surprisingly, because Cottesloe is the birthplace of surfing and surf lifesaving in Western Australia, people go from all over the globe to surf its waves every day. If you consider yourself a good surfer, enjoy lines of left- and right-hand waves by paddling out to the groyne. If you've never surfed before, go for the quiet waves in the middle of the beach or take lessons at nearby Leighton Beach.

Laze along the promenade
The Cottesloe Esplanade is a wonderful location for picnics or simply taking in the ocean view because of its wide stretch of grass and tall Norfolk Pine trees that provide shade. Admire the magnificent Cottesloe sunset, drift off to the sounds of rainbow lorikeets, and maybe catch a live outdoor music performance on the grass.

Take part in swimming the Rottnest Channel, or just watch
The Rottnest Channel Swim is not something to be undertaken by the timid. Swimmers meet at Cottesloe Beach in February to start their 20-kilometer (12-mile) swim across open seas to Rottnest Island. Athletes may swim alone, in pairs, or teams. Visitors may make a whole day of it since there are family-friendly activities and entertainment scheduled throughout the day.

Travel around lovely routes.
One of the best ways to experience Perth is while riding a bike. Rent an e-bike in Cottesloe and choose your journey. The Cottesloe to Hillary cycling trail, which spans 25 km (16 mi), provides stunning views of Perth's coastline. Alternatively, the 16 km (10 mi) Bush to Beach trail takes you directly into the center

of the city while passing through parklands rich in historic heritage.

Location: Marine Parade, 6011, Cottesloe, Western Australia

CITY BEACH

Free Admission

City Beach has often been named Perth's greatest beach in recent years because of its lovely stretches of white sand and first-rate amenities. In addition to providing safe swimming for the entire family, two specially constructed groynes provide fantastic fishing, and surfers often pound the waves close offshore.

Summertime surf lifesaving carnivals are held regularly at City Beach. Watch as Australian surf life rescuers demonstrate their abilities.

City Beach has well-kept outdoor spaces with picnic tables, grills, and children's play area in addition to restrooms, showers, and changing places.

Additionally, there is a fine dining restaurant with a view of the ocean and a kiosk. As the sun sets over the Indian Ocean, savor a glass of wine from Western Australia that has won several awards. Or light up the grill at dark, just as the natives do.

Perth's affluent, ultra-modern homes may be seen in City Beach, where verdant green spaces provide an opulent background.

City Beach, which is around a 15-minute drive from Perth, has lots of parking.

Location: City Beach, Western Australia, 6015 West Coast Highway

SCARBOROUGH BEACH

For teens and surfers, Scarborough Beach is a firm favourite. The regular swell, impressive surf breaks and long stretch of white sand attract swimmers, surfers and body-boarders. Scarborough Beach is also popular for kite surfing and windsurfing, especially when the afternoon sea breeze is in.

At night, Scarborough's foreshore comes alive. There are many restaurants and cafes to choose from, or you can pack a picnic and enjoy the large grassed areas, public barbecues and gazebos.

Brand new to the Scarborough Beach landscape is the Scarborough Beach Pool, a geo-thermally heated open-air public pool and world-class recreation facility. It's your go-to fitness centre and your new local eatery - the perfect place to visit all year round.

Scarborough Beach also features an outdoor amphitheatre which in summer hosts all kinds of events including beach cricket.

There's plenty of accommodation along this stretch of coast, making Scarborough Beach an ideal place for a summer holiday.

Surf Life Savers are regularly on patrol at Scarborough Beach ensuring the safety of the public.

Scarborough Beach is about a 20-minute drive northwest of Perth and regular buses run from the city.

Entry cost
Free

Location
via West Coast Highway, Scarborough, Western Australia, 6019

Activities
Birdwatching, Cycling, Fishing, Scenic Drives, Scuba Diving, Snorkelling, Surfing, Swimming, Walks.

BEST SURFING SPOTS

1. Scarborough Beach
Known for its consistent swell and laid-back vibe, it's a favorite among both locals and visitors. The beach boasts reliable waves year-round, making it ideal for intermediate to advanced surfers. Scarborough is also home to various surf schools, so beginners can learn the ropes in a friendly, supportive environment. After a surf session, the area around the beach offers plenty of cafes, bars, and shops where you can relax and refuel.

2. Trigg Beach
Just north of Scarborough, Trigg Beach is another prime surf location. Trigg's reef breaks make it a go-to spot for more experienced surfers looking for challenging conditions. The waves here tend to be a bit more powerful and consistent, especially in the winter months, when swells are larger. Trigg Point, in particular, is known for producing great barrels. If you're a skilled

surfer looking for some exciting rides, this is the place to be. There's also a quieter, gentler area for beginners just south of the main break.

3. Cottesloe Beach

Cottesloe Beach is famous for its white sands and crystal-clear waters, and while it's more commonly known as a swimming beach, it can offer some decent waves on the right day. When the swell hits, Cottesloe becomes a great spot for beginner to intermediate surfers, with gentler waves that are ideal for practicing and refining your skills. Plus, the beautiful surroundings and nearby cafes make it a great spot to spend a whole day at the beach, whether you're surfing or simply soaking up the sun.

4. Leighton Beach

If you're looking for a more laid-back surfing experience, Leighton Beach is the place to go. Located just south of Cottesloe, Leighton is known for its mellow waves, making it a perfect spot for beginners and longboarders. The beach features wide, sandy stretches and plenty of space, so it's never too crowded, even on the weekends. Leighton's gentle conditions make it an ideal place to start learning how to surf or to enjoy a relaxed session on a smaller swell day.

5. Secret Harbour

For those willing to venture a bit farther south of Perth, Secret Harbour offers some of the best and most consistent surf conditions in the region. Located about 45 minutes from the city center, Secret Harbour is a popular spot for surfers looking to escape the crowds. The beach breaks here are powerful, with long, clean waves that are perfect for intermediate and advanced surfers. The area is also less developed than other Perth beaches, giving it a more natural and peaceful atmosphere, perfect for those looking to focus on their surf.

6. Rottnest Island

A short ferry ride from Perth, Rottnest Island offers some of the best surfing conditions in the region, thanks to its exposure to bigger swells from the Indian Ocean. There are several breaks around the island, catering to all levels of surfers. Strickland Bay, in particular, is renowned for its powerful, hollow waves and is a favorite among advanced surfers. Other spots like **The Basin** offer more gentle breaks, making them suitable for beginners. Surfing at Rottnest Island is a unique experience, combining epic waves with the island's stunning natural beauty and abundant wildlife, including the famous quokkas.

7. City Beach

Close to the city center, City Beach is a convenient surf spot that offers a decent swell, especially during the winter months. While it's not as challenging as some of the more famous surf beaches in Perth, City Beach is a great option for those looking for a quick surf session without traveling too far. The waves are generally friendly to beginners and intermediate surfers, and the beach is well-patrolled, making it a safe spot to enjoy the water.

CULTURAL AND HISTORICAL LANDMARKS

PERTH CULTURAL CENTRE

The arts, culture, knowledge, and community are all brought together at the Perth Cultural Centre.

The city's cultural center is a place to take in the sunlight, utilize the free WiFi, and participate in the activities scheduled and Perth events.

Situated near public transportation and serving as a critical link between Northbridge's retail, food and beverage, and entertainment zone and the Perth CBD, the Cultural Centre has seen a metamorphosis from an underutilized area to a vibrant public place.

The Perth Cultural Centre is home to the major educational, cultural, and artistic institutions in the State, such as:

1. Western Australian Art Gallery

2. Museum of Western Australia

3. Western Australian State Library

4. The Perth Institute of Contemporary Arts

5. The Blue Room Theatre

6. Western Australia's State Theatre Centre

7. State Records Office of the Central Institute of Technology

Opposite the WA Museum Boola Bardip lies the unique tiny playspace, Perth Cultural Centre Playspace, which emphasizes sensory play. The Perth Cultural Centre Playspace blends art and nature with interactive elements that children may handle and investigate, such as rotating wheels and wood sculptures. Perfectly crafted with organic hues and textures, it exudes a serene vibe even in the heart of the metropolis.

For further information, please visit the website. The Center is also accessible for events.

Address: William and James Street, Perth, Western Australia, 6000

Please call (08) 6557 0700.

Open Hours: Round-the-clock

AUSTRALIA'S WESTERN ART GALLERY

The Art Gallery of Western Australia (AGWA), the state's center for visual arts, is located in the center of the Perth Cultural Centre.

Situated in a globally recognized Brutalist structure crafted by Architect Charles Sierakowski, AGWA has an outstanding assemblage of artworks by artists of First Nations and Western Australian descent, in addition to pieces from other parts of Australia and beyond.

With one of the biggest rooftop areas in Western Australia, AGWA's new rooftop refurbishment offers a rooftop bar, event space, and an outdoor sculpture promenade that overlooks Perth's breathtaking metropolitan skyline and the 34-meter-long, lighting artwork by Noongar artist Christopher Pease.

Beside the new is one of the oldest structures in Washington, dating back to 1905—the former police courts. These historically significant "Centenary Galleries" are now hosting a rotating series of shows.

Throughout the year, AGWA presents a wide range of exhibits along with a vibrant calendar of activities that includes music, performance art, artist lectures, and more.

A visit to the Gallery's Design Store, which is renowned for carrying cutting-edge design items by regional and worldwide artists, would not be complete without perusing the exquisite design, craft, and art objects on display.

The Gallery is open every day except Christmas Day, Good Friday, and Tuesdays. All ages are welcome, and contributions are accepted. Certain special exhibits could need reservations.

The address is Perth Cultural Centre, Perth, WA 6000.

Call (08) 9492-6600.

Open Wednesday through Monday from 10 a.m. to 5 p.m.; closed on Tuesdays, Good Friday, and Christmas Day.

PRISON FREMANTLE

One of the most popular tourist destinations and cultural heritage sites in Western Australia is Fremantle Prison. It is the only structure in the state to be included on the World Heritage List and the only site in the Perth metropolitan area to be inscribed on the list.

Convicts constructed Fremantle Prison in the 1850s, and it was utilized as a jail for 136 years until it was shut down in 1991 as an operational maximum security facility.

On a variety of engaging tours, guests may "step inside and do time" with the knowledgeable guides of Fremantle Prison. Tours like "Behind Bars," "Convict Prison," and "True Crime" showcase prison and prisoner life, spectacular escapes, and colorful personalities in stories with a hint of humor from inside the jail. Adventure-seeking guests may go 20 meters below the jail to explore a one-kilometer maze of tunnels on foot and by boat as part of a "Tunnels Tour," or take a creepy "Torchlight Tour" at night to learn more about the darkest aspects of the prison's past.

Apart from providing guided tours, Fremantle Prison offers other amenities including an award-winning gift store, an educational Visitor Center, an onsite café, and exhibits in the Prison Gallery.

Daily opening hours: 9 a.m. to 5 p.m.

Wednesday, 9 a.m. to 9:30 p.m.
Friday: 9:00 am–9:30 pm
Christmas Day: Not Open; April 18: Not Open
Christmas Day: Not Open

Admission price
Tickets for all: $22 to $65
Children: between $12 and $45

Address: 1 The Terrace; Phone: +61 8 9336 9200; Fremantle, Western Australia, 6160

THE PERTH MINT

One of the top tourist attractions in Perth is the Perth Mint, which is also the oldest mint in operation in Australia.

The Perth Mint and the history of Western Australian gold are brought to life in its top-notch exhibition rooms, allowing visitors to feel the allure of gold.

Watch a classic gold pour at the Mint's historic 1899 melting house, and take in the sight of the biggest coin in the world, weighing one tonne of pure gold and worth over $70 million, which holds the Guinness World Record. Experience handling gold bullion valued at over $700,000 and see the minting of precious metal coins right in front of your eyes.

Create your medallion to find out how much gold is in you. You may also buy special treasures from Western Australia, such as beautiful South Sea pearls and Argyle pink diamonds. (Sales are offered tax-free).

After the tour, unwind in the outside café with a cup of tea or coffee and a little snack.

The address is 310 Hay Street East, Perth, WA 60004.

Please call (08) 9421 7376.

Operating Hours
Open every day
Hourly tours are available from 9.30 am until 3.30 pm.

DAY TRIPS FROM PERTH

ROTTNEST ISLAND

A day trip to Rottnest Island from Perth is a perfect escape for nature lovers, beachgoers, and wildlife enthusiasts. Located just 19 kilometers off the coast of Perth, Rottnest Island offers a serene and picturesque getaway, famed for its pristine beaches, crystal-clear waters, and adorable quokkas, small marsupials that are native to the island. The island's laid-back vibe, rich history, and natural beauty make it a must-visit destination.

Getting to Rottnest Island
The journey to Rottnest Island begins with a ferry ride from either Fremantle, Perth City, or Hillarys Boat Harbour. The ferry ride takes about 25 minutes from Fremantle and around 90 minutes from Perth City, providing scenic views of the coastline along the way. Ferries operate frequently throughout the day, so it's easy to plan a day trip that fits your schedule.

Exploring the Island: Meet the Quokkas
Upon arrival, one of the island's main attractions awaits—the quokka. Often referred to as the "happiest animal in the world," quokkas are small, friendly marsupials with natural smiles that have captured the hearts of travelers. The best spots to see quokkas are near the main settlement and around the cafes, where these curious creatures often gather. While they are wild animals, quokkas are very approachable, and many visitors snap selfies with them. However, it's important to remember not to feed or touch them, as they are protected by law.

Beaches and Snorkeling
Rottnest Island boasts some of the most beautiful beaches in Australia, perfect for swimming, sunbathing, and snorkeling. The island is home to over 60 picturesque beaches and 20 stunning bays, each offering unique views and activities.

- The Basin: Just a short walk from the ferry terminal, The Basin is one of the island's most famous beaches. Its calm, shallow waters make it ideal for families and those looking for a relaxing swim.
- Little Salmon Bay: Known for its vibrant underwater life, this beach is perfect for snorkeling. Colorful fish and corals can be seen just a few meters from the shore.
- Pinky Beach: Located near Bathurst Lighthouse, Pinky Beach is another popular spot where you can unwind on soft white sand and take in breathtaking ocean views.

Cycling and Exploring
Rottnest Island is car-free, so the best way to explore the island is by bicycle. You can rent a bike near the ferry terminal or bring your own on the ferry. Cycling offers a fantastic way to see the island at your own pace, allowing you to visit secluded beaches and scenic lookouts that aren't accessible by foot. Popular cycling routes take you around the island's 22 kilometers of coastal roads, offering stunning views at every turn.

For those interested in history, the island is home to several heritage sites, including the Wadjemup Lighthouse, Oliver Hill Battery, and World War II-era tunnels. You can also take guided tours to learn more about the island's indigenous heritage and colonial history.

Wildlife and Natural Beauty
In addition to quokkas, Rottnest Island is teeming with wildlife. Keep an eye out for various bird species, including ospreys and seagulls, as well as marine life like dolphins and sea lions, which can often be spotted around the island's coastline. If you're lucky, you might even see humpback whales during their migration season between September and November.

Dining and Relaxation
After a day of exploring, there are several cafes and restaurants on the island where you can refuel. The main settlement offers a variety of dining options, from casual fish and chips to more upscale meals with ocean views. Alternatively, you can bring your picnic and enjoy a meal on one of the many beaches or grassy picnic areas scattered across the island.

SWAN VALLEY WINE REGION

Just a short drive from the bustling streets of Perth, the Swan Valley Wine Region presents a delightful escape into Western Australia's oldest wine-producing area. Renowned for its refined wineries, boutique breweries, and gourmet eateries, this scenic valley is the perfect destination for a day trip filled with indulgence and relaxation.

Start your journey with a leisurely drive along the Swan Valley Food and Wine Trail. This 32-kilometer loop is dotted with more than 150 attractions including wineries, distilleries, restaurants, cafes, and artisan shops. Each stop offers a unique slice of the region's rich culinary heritage. Don't miss sampling the locally produced Verdelho, a specialty of the valley, which is a must-try for wine aficionados.

One of the highlights of your trip should be a visit to some of the family-run wineries where the winemakers themselves often conduct tastings and share insights into their winemaking process. Savor the complexity of flavors in each glass, accompanied by expertly paired cheeses and charcuterie.

For lunch, choose from one of the many vineyard cafes offering picturesque views over lush green vineyards. Indulge in dishes prepared with fresh local produce, showcasing the flavors of the region.

After lunch, consider exploring the Swan Valley's rich cultural landscape. Visit the local aboriginal gallery to appreciate indigenous art and history or stop by one of the craft studios to witness glass blowing and pottery making.

Before heading back to Perth, make sure to stop at the Chocolate Company and the Nougat Factory to pick up some sweet treats for the road. The region is also famous for its honey and handmade soaps, making it easy to bring a piece of Swan Valley back home with you.

A day trip to Swan Valley is not just a journey through a wine lover's paradise but also a deep dive into the culinary and cultural delights of Western Australia. Whether you're a seasoned wine connoisseur or a casual tourist, Swan Valley offers an enriching experience that tantalizes the senses and soothes the soul.

PINNACLES DESERT

Day Trip to Pinnacles Desert from Perth
Embark on a surreal adventure from Perth to the Pinnacles Desert, a unique natural wonder located in the heart of Nambung National Park. This day trip offers a striking contrast from the urban landscape of Perth, presenting an ancient desert sprinkled with thousands of limestone spires that rise mysteriously from the yellow sands.

Begin your journey early from Perth, heading north for about two hours to reach the Pinnacles Desert. The drive itself is scenic, offering views of Australia's rugged coastline and expansive wildflower displays during the spring months.

Upon arriving in the desert, you can explore the Pinnacles on foot or by car. The desert has an accessible loop that lets visitors drive around and stop at various points to wander among the limestone formations. These structures, some standing as high as 3.5 meters, create a striking visual spectacle against the stark blue sky. Walking paths and viewing platforms are available for those who prefer to explore the area on foot, providing closer encounters with the formations and the wildlife that inhabits the area, including kangaroos and emus.

Next, visit the Pinnacles Desert Discovery Centre, where you can learn about the geology of the formations, the cultural history of the area, and the biodiversity of the park. The interactive displays and informative panels offer insights into how the Pinnacles were formed and the indigenous significance of the land.

For a break, head to the nearby town of Cervantes, a quaint coastal village where you can enjoy fresh seafood for lunch. The Lobster Shack offers tours of their lobster processing plant complemented by a fresh seafood platter, giving you a taste of the local catch.

In the afternoon, consider extending your exploration to the beautiful beaches of the Turquoise Coast, like Hangover Bay and Kangaroo Point, which are perfect for swimming and snorkeling. These spots are also great for relaxing and soaking in the serene coastal ambiance before heading back to Perth.

A day trip to the Pinnacles Desert offers not only a glimpse into Australia's natural history but also an opportunity to witness one of the most visually striking landscapes. This unique geological feature, combined with the rich cultural and marine experiences nearby, makes for an unforgettable adventure just a short drive from Perth.

MARGARET RIVER REGION

A day trip to the Margaret River Region from Perth is a fantastic way to explore one of Western Australia's most renowned destinations, known for its natural beauty, wine, and gourmet experiences. Though it's a 2.5 to 3-hour drive south of Perth, the journey itself is scenic and rewarding.

Getting There
Leaving Perth early in the morning, you'll travel along the Kwinana Freeway before joining the Forrest Highway and Bussell Highway. Along the way, you may choose to stop in towns like

Bunbury or Busselton for a quick coffee break or to visit the iconic Busselton Jetty, one of the longest wooden jetties in the world.

Wine and Gourmet Delights
The Margaret River Region is famed for its wineries, producing some of Australia's best Cabernet Sauvignon and Chardonnay. Upon arrival, you can visit a selection of the area's world-class wineries, such as Leeuwin Estate, Vasse Felix, or Voyager Estate. Many of these wineries offer tastings, cellar door experiences, and vineyard tours. Pair your wine experience with a lunch stop at a winery restaurant, where local produce is elevated to gourmet dishes.

If wine isn't your primary interest, the region also boasts numerous craft breweries, distilleries, and even chocolate and cheese factories. A visit to Margaret River Chocolate Company or the Margaret River Dairy Company will satisfy any cravings for sweets or cheese.

Natural Attractions
Beyond food and drink, the region is home to stunning natural attractions. Spend part of your day exploring the coastal beauty of the region at Cape Naturaliste or Cape Leeuwin, where the Indian and Southern Oceans meet. You can walk part of the Cape to Cape Track for breathtaking coastal views or visit one of the area's famous caves, such as Lake Cave or Jewel Cave, to see stunning subterranean formations.

Beaches and Adventure
The Margaret River Region's beaches are another highlight. Stop at Surfers Point near Prevelly to watch surfers take on the

massive swells, or take a dip at Gnarabup Beach for a more relaxing swim. For those keen on adventure, there are plenty of options, including whale watching (seasonal), stand-up paddleboarding, and hiking in the surrounding forests.

Return to Perth

By late afternoon, begin your return journey to Perth. If you have time, a stop at the small town of Cowaramup, known for its quirky cow-themed sculptures, can add a light-hearted touch to your trip. Alternatively, stop for dinner at one of the charming restaurants along the Bussell Highway before making your way back to the city in the evening.

BEST OUTDOOR ACTIVITIES

HIKING TRAILS AROUND PERTH

Perth is home to an abundance of natural beauty, with numerous hiking trails that offer breathtaking landscapes, from coastal paths to forested hills.

1. Kings Park and Botanic Garden
Just minutes from the city center, Kings Park offers several walking and hiking trails through its 400 hectares of bushland and gardens. The Law Walk, a 2.5 km trail, provides stunning views of the Swan River and the city skyline. The Bushland Nature Trail is another popular option, offering a serene escape into native flora and fauna, right in the heart of Perth.

2. John Forrest National Park
One of Western Australia's oldest national parks, John Forrest is located just 24 km east of Perth. It offers a variety of hiking options, from the Eagle View Walk, a challenging 15 km loop trail through woodlands and valleys, to shorter trails like the Railway Reserve Heritage Trail, which follows the path of a disused railway line and is ideal for a more relaxed experience. Along the way, you'll encounter waterfalls, wildlife, and stunning views of the city.

3. Bibbulmun Track
For more adventurous hikers, the Bibbulmun Track is one of the world's great long-distance trails, stretching over 1,000 km from the Perth Hills to Albany on the south coast. While a full thru-hike

takes weeks, many sections of the track are accessible for day hikes. The Mundaring to Kalamunda section, just 30 minutes from Perth, offers beautiful forested trails and views over valleys, making it a popular day hike.

4. Lesmurdie Falls

Located in the Darling Range, just 30 minutes from the city, the Lesmurdie Falls National Park offers several walking trails that take you to the base and summit of the falls. The Falls Trail is a 2 km loop, while the Lesmurdie Brook Loop offers a slightly longer 3 km hike through bushland. The highlight is the impressive waterfall, especially after rain, with panoramic views of the Perth plains from the top.

5. Bold Park

Situated near the coast, Bold Park offers a network of trails that range from easy to moderate. The Reabold Hill Walk, a 2.1 km loop, leads you to one of the highest natural points in the metropolitan area, providing sweeping views of Perth, the Indian Ocean, and Rottnest Island. The Zamia Trail is another 5 km track that winds through the park's diverse vegetation, ideal for birdwatching.

CYCLING ROUTES

Perth is known for its cycling-friendly infrastructure, with a range of scenic routes that cater to both casual riders and cycling enthusiasts. From coastal paths to riverside rides, the city's diverse routes provide cyclists with the perfect way to explore.

1. Swan River Loop

One of the most iconic cycling routes in Perth, the Swan River Loop is a 10 km to 30 km ride (depending on where you start) that takes you along the picturesque Swan River. The loop can start at various points, including Elizabeth Quay or South Perth, and offers easy cycling with plenty of cafes and scenic spots along the way. The flat, well-maintained paths make it suitable for all levels of cyclists.

2. City to Fremantle
For a longer ride, the City to Fremantle route spans around 30 km and takes you from central Perth along the southern banks of the Swan River to the historic port city of Fremantle. The ride passes through several beautiful parks and riverside suburbs, with plenty of opportunities to stop and enjoy the views. Once in Fremantle, you can explore the bustling markets, heritage buildings, and beaches.

3. Loch Street to Cottesloe Beach
This shorter 6 km ride offers an enjoyable route from Loch Street Station to Cottesloe Beach, one of Perth's most famous beaches. The route is a gentle ride through leafy suburbs and concludes with breathtaking ocean views at Cottesloe, where you can relax on the sandy shores or grab a coffee at one of the beachside cafes.

4. Perth to Hillarys
Cyclists looking for a coastal ride will love the Perth to Hillarys route, which is around 30 km each way. Starting from the Perth CBD, the route heads west towards Scarborough Beach and then follows the coastal path north, taking in pristine beaches and ocean views. Hillarys Boat Harbour is a popular end-point, where

you can explore shops, grab a bite to eat, or even take a dip in the sheltered waters.

5. Kep Track

For those looking to combine nature with cycling, the Kep Track offers a fantastic off-road experience. Running between Mundaring and Northam, this 75 km track follows the old railway line and is ideal for mountain biking. The track passes through forested areas, open farmland, and small towns, offering a unique glimpse into the rural side of Western Australia.

WILDLIFE AND NATURE RESERVES IN PERTH

Perth is home to an abundance of wildlife and nature reserves, offering visitors the chance to experience Australia's unique flora and fauna.

1. Yanchep National Park

Located about 50 km north of Perth, Yanchep National Park is one of the best spots to experience Australian wildlife in a natural setting. The park is home to a wide variety of animals, including koalas, western grey kangaroos, and abundant birdlife. One of the main attractions is the Koala Boardwalk, where you can observe koalas in their natural habitat. There are also several walking trails through the park's wetlands and bushland, where you might encounter echidnas, black swans, and native plants such as wildflowers during spring.

2. Caversham Wildlife Park

For those wanting an up-close encounter with Australian wildlife, Caversham Wildlife Park, located in the Whiteman Park conservation area, offers a family-friendly experience. Visitors can hand-feed kangaroos, and pet wombats, and see a range of other native animals, including dingoes, emus, and Tasmanian devils. The park also provides interactive experiences like sheep shearing and meet-and-greet sessions with koalas. The surrounding Whiteman Park is a nature reserve in itself, offering picnic areas, walking paths, and natural bushland to explore.

3. Penguin Island

Just 45 minutes south of Perth, Penguin Island is home to the world's smallest penguins, the little penguins. A short ferry ride from Rockingham will take you to this small island, where you can view these adorable creatures in their natural habitat or at the Discovery Centre. The island also supports a colony of sea lions and offers great opportunities for birdwatching, including pelicans, ospreys, and a variety of seabirds. Nature trails crisscross the island, making it an ideal spot for a day of wildlife viewing and scenic walks.

4. Herdsman Lake Regional Park

Located just 7 km from the Perth CBD, Herdsman Lake is an important wetland reserve, home to over 100 species of birds. The park offers a peaceful setting for birdwatching, with opportunities to spot species such as black swans, pelicans, ibis, and a variety of waterbirds. There are also walking and cycling paths around the lake, allowing visitors to explore the diverse plant life and wetlands that support a variety of reptiles and amphibians.

5. Bold Park

Just a short drive from the city center, Bold Park is a 437-hectare urban wilderness, offering a refuge for native flora and fauna. The park's Zamia Trail provides a 5 km walk through diverse vegetation, and it's a great spot to observe native bird species, including honeyeaters, parrots, and kookaburras. The park is also home to several reptile species and is a fantastic place for nature lovers to enjoy Perth's coastal bushland and panoramic views of the city and ocean.

RIVER CRUISES ON THE SWAN RIVER

The Swan River is the lifeblood of Perth, winding through the heart of the city and offering scenic views of the skyline, waterfront, and surrounding nature. One of the best ways to experience the beauty of Perth's river is by taking a river cruise, providing a relaxing and informative journey through the city's iconic waterway.

1. City Sights and Scenic Cruises
For a leisurely way to explore the river, city sights cruises depart regularly from Barrack Street Jetty, taking visitors on a scenic loop around Perth's waterfront. These cruises offer panoramic views of landmarks such as Kings Park, the Old Swan Brewery, and the city's modern skyline. Commentary is often provided, giving insights into Perth's history and the significance of the Swan River to the region. These cruises are ideal for those wanting a short and relaxed introduction to Perth from the water.

2. Perth to Fremantle Cruises
A popular option for visitors is the Perth to Fremantle cruise, which travels along the Swan River to the historic port city of

Fremantle. This journey offers a blend of urban and natural sights, passing luxury riverside homes, yacht clubs, and pristine parks. The cruise typically lasts around 75 minutes and provides stunning views of the riverbanks, dotted with pelicans, dolphins, and other wildlife. Upon arrival in Fremantle, passengers can explore the town's markets, museums, and beaches before catching a return ferry or continuing their journey.

3. Swan Valley Wine Cruises

For wine enthusiasts, a Swan Valley wine cruise is a must. Departing from central Perth, these cruises head upstream to the Swan Valley, a renowned wine region. Onboard, passengers can enjoy tastings of local wines and gourmet snacks, with some cruises including stops at riverside wineries for lunch and vineyard tours. The return journey is a relaxing ride back down the river as the sun sets over the city, making it a perfect day out for those looking to combine sightseeing with culinary indulgence.

4. Wildlife and Eco-Cruises

For a more nature-focused experience, eco cruises on the Swan River offer opportunities to spot local wildlife, including dolphins, black swans, and other bird species that inhabit the riverbanks. These eco-friendly cruises are often guided by knowledgeable local experts who provide insights into the river's ecology, conservation efforts, and the indigenous cultural significance of the waterway. These cruises offer a peaceful way to explore the quieter parts of the Swan River while learning about its diverse ecosystem.

5. Twilight and Dinner Cruises

For a romantic or special evening, twilight cruises and dinner cruises on the Swan River provide a memorable experience. As the sun sets over the river, these cruises offer breathtaking views of Perth's illuminated skyline. Dinner cruises often include a multi-course meal, live entertainment, and the chance to enjoy the serene beauty of the river by night. Whether you're celebrating a special occasion or just want a unique dining experience, these evening cruises offer a perfect blend of sightseeing and fine dining.

SHOPPING IN PERTH

HAY STREET MALL AND MURRAY STREET MALL

Located in the heart of Perth's bustling central business district, Hay Street Mall and Murray Street Mall are two of the city's most popular shopping destinations. These pedestrian-friendly malls are packed with a variety of shops, boutiques, and department stores, offering something for every type of shopper.

Hay Street Mall
Hay Street Mall is one of Perth's premier shopping streets, offering a mix of international brands, local retailers, and specialty stores. This outdoor mall stretches between Barrack and William Streets and is well-known for its wide array of fashion, beauty, and lifestyle offerings.

- High-End and Popular Brands: Hay Street Mall is home to many well-known international retailers, such as Zara, Swarovski, and H&M. For those looking to splurge, luxury brands like Michael Kors and Omega have flagship stores here, catering to more exclusive tastes.

- Local Fashion and Boutiques: In addition to global brands, the mall also features local Australian fashion labels and independent boutiques, offering visitors a chance to pick up something unique. Stores such as Cue, Witchery, and Gorman showcase the best in contemporary Australian design, blending high-quality craftsmanship with on-trend styles.

- Department Stores: David Jones, one of Australia's leading department stores, is a key anchor in Hay Street Mall. Here, shoppers can find a wide selection of designer clothing, accessories, cosmetics, and homeware all under one roof, making it a convenient stop for those wanting a more comprehensive shopping experience.

Murray Street Mall
Running parallel to Hay Street, Murray Street Mall is another prime shopping destination, offering a lively atmosphere with a slightly more casual, family-friendly vibe. It is also a pedestrian-only area, making it ideal for a relaxed shopping day.

- Mainstream Retailers: Murray Street Mall features popular high-street brands like Myer, Uniqlo, and Foot Locker, making it the go-to spot for everyday fashion, footwear, and accessories. Whether you're looking for the latest styles or everyday essentials, the stores here cater to a wide range of tastes and budgets.

- Tech and Gadgets: Tech enthusiasts will enjoy browsing JB Hi-Fi and Apple Store, both located in Murray Street Mall. These stores offer the latest in gadgets, electronics, and accessories, making them perfect stops for anyone interested in tech.

- Cafes and Eateries: After a few hours of shopping, the mall also offers various cafes and eateries where visitors can take a break and enjoy a coffee or a quick bite to eat. Gloria Jean's Coffees and Hudsons Coffee are popular spots for grabbing a drink, while food courts inside the nearby Carillon City and Forrest Chase offer a variety of dining options.

Shopping Atmosphere and Surroundings
Both Hay Street and Murray Street Malls are vibrant and pedestrian-only, ensuring a pleasant shopping experience free from traffic. The two malls are lined with street performers, buskers, and occasional pop-up market stalls, creating a lively and engaging atmosphere. The architecture in the area blends modern storefronts with historic buildings, giving the malls a unique charm.

Additional Shopping Hubs Nearby
Just steps away from these malls, shoppers can explore other shopping precincts like Forrest Chase, Carillon City, and Enex 100, all of which offer even more retail options. Forrest Chase is home to Myer and a selection of smaller specialty stores, while Enex 100 offers a mix of fashion, food, and beauty stores in a sleek, modern setting.

Getting There
Conveniently located in Perth's CBD, Hay Street and Murray Street Malls are easily accessible via public transport. Both malls are a short walk from Perth Train Station and are well-serviced by the city's bus routes, including the free CAT buses that operate in the central area. Paid parking is available at nearby car parks for those driving into the city.

KING STREET: HIGH-END SHOPPING

King Street is renowned as Perth's premier destination for luxury shopping, offering an upscale and refined retail experience. Located in the heart of the city, this historic street is home to a variety of high-end fashion boutiques, jewelry stores, and designer brands, catering to both locals and international visitors seeking exclusive items.

The street exudes a sense of elegance, with beautifully restored heritage buildings that house world-famous designer names such as Chanel, Gucci, Prada, and Louis Vuitton. It's a haven for fashion enthusiasts, where stylish window displays showcase the latest collections, drawing in shoppers looking for timeless pieces and the season's must-haves.

Apart from fashion, King Street is also the place to find bespoke jewelry and luxury watches from brands like Cartier and Rolex. Whether you're searching for a signature piece of jewelry or the latest in luxury timepieces, King Street's selection offers a blend of craftsmanship and sophistication.

Beyond shopping, the atmosphere on King Street adds to the experience. The tree-lined avenue is dotted with chic cafes and gourmet eateries, providing the perfect spots for a leisurely break in between shopping. It's a place where one can enjoy a luxurious day out, combining the best of retail therapy with gourmet delights.

King Street's central location makes it easily accessible and an essential stop for those seeking Perth's finest shopping experience. Whether you're a local or a visitor, the street offers an unmatched glimpse into the high-end lifestyle, where style and elegance converge in the city's most fashionable district.

PERTH'S BEST MARKETS

Perth Upscale
Where: Winthrop Hall, University of Western Australia, 35 Stirling Highway, Crawley
When: Listed here, every three months.

Known for its handcrafted items and independent designers, this specialized market takes place four times a year. This event, which takes place at Winthrop Hall in the lush surroundings of the University of Western Australia, brings together over 180 artists, crafters, and culinary experts. There are certain to be unique things at the market, which was established to promote local business and assist Western Australian artists.

Farmers Market in Freo
Where: 79 Lefroy Road, Beaconsfield, Fremantle College
When: 8 am to 12 pm on Sunday

On Sundays, the Freo Farmers Market is held in Beaconsfield, a suburb in Perth's south. Under the towering eucalyptus trees, stalls are scattered with fruit that is directly from the farmer and locally made goods. Along with jams and fresh flowers, you can discover organic meats, free-range eggs, locally squeezed olive oil, crisp bread, and honey from the area. Keep in mind that the market does not accept plastic bags. Live acoustic music contributes to the laid-back vibe of the neighborhood.

City Farm in Perth
Where: East Perth's 1 City Farm Place
When: 8 a.m.–12 p.m. on Saturday

Popular Perth City Farm is a haven for lovers of all things ecological, ethical, biodynamic, and organic. No chemical sprays are applied to the fruit, vegetables, dairy, raw honey, or meats. Organic apparel, health foods, and body care items are also available. The farm is next to a great café with rich chocolate and raspberry cake, creamy scrambled eggs, and strong coffee. Because it is enclosed, the market may be difficult to locate. In East Perth, it is located behind a large asphalt parking lot on Royal Street. Alternatively, you can take the rail to Claisebrook station and locate it from the pedestrian bridge.

The Night Markets at Inglewood
Where: Inglewood, 892/894 Beaufort St.
When: Mondays, September through March, 6 to 9:30 p.m.

Monday evenings are when many cities close. However, Inglewood, a suburb of Perth, is thriving, with food trucks supplying hungry residents with food along the lengthy Beaufort Street promenade that runs between Sixth and Eleventh avenues. Situated only three miles or five kilometers from the city center, it's a great place to select your supper and take in the lively atmosphere. For the buskers, who contribute to the atmosphere, pack a few gold coins.

Farmers Market in Subi
Where: 271 Bagot Road, Subiaco; Subiaco Primary School
When: 8 a.m.–12 p.m. on Saturday

Located in Subiaco, a well-known urban suburb in Perth, the Subi Farmers Market is bustling with friends meeting up as they choose punnets of strawberries and freshly baked bread or wait in line for Moroccan eggs, known as shakshuka. The grounds of Subiaco Primary School are the venue for the market. Locals like having coffee and something to eat beneath the large fig tree while watching their children play nearby.

Farmers Market at Mount Claremont
Where: 103 Alfred Road, Mount Claremont; Mt. Claremont Primary School
When: 7:30 am to 11:30 am on Saturday

This is best suited for avid eaters. At the Mount Claremont Farmers Market, premium seasonal food is displayed alongside booths with artisan cheeses, gourmet meats, French pastries, and cut flowers. Naturally, the prices correspond with the quality of the product. That's not to argue that you can't find a good deal. For instance, the lettuce truck often sells out ahead of schedule and offers excellent value greens, such as watercress, bunches of coriander, and cleaned baby butter leaf. Christmas stone fruit is very delicious.

Fremantle Markets
Where: Henderson Street and South Terrace, Fremantle
When: 8 am to 6 pm on Friday, Saturday, and Sunday

in least 150 vendors offering fresh fruit, street food, art, home goods, toys, and more can be found in the historic Fremantle Markets. Built-in 1897, the markets are a gorgeous jumble of hues, scents, and mementos all beneath one enormous roof. In addition to the ephemera, you may also discover mementos that will last a lifetime, such as panoramic shots of Perth's white sand beaches, emu oil that soothes your skin, and the hammock of your dreams. Hurry to The Yard just before closing for aggressively advertised, deeply priced produce.

LOCAL SOUVENIRS TO BUY

Perth's souvenir stores provide unforgettable presents that go beyond the typical t-shirts, shot glasses, and fridge door magnets. So instead of settling for the same old souvenirs, explore the unique artwork, premium wines, and cuddly animals that Perth has to offer.

Indigenous Art
Because of its distinctive style and wide range of aesthetics, Aboriginal artworks and artifacts have been a major export from the nation since the British colonized the area over 30,000 years ago. Because of this, out of all the Perth souvenirs, this is the one to think of giving.

Some items could be more appropriate for a traveler wanting to breeze through customs, but a didgeridoo might be a bit difficult to get on the aircraft (but we don't discourage you from bringing this back since it makes a wonderful present). Printmaking, textile art, paintings, weavings, sculpture, and rock carvings are all excellent keepsakes from Perth that honor Australia's rich and priceless Aboriginal past.

Visit these Perth souvenir stores to see some amazing unique artwork:

Gallery Japingka. 47 on the High Street. opens at ten in the morning.

Perth's Creative Natives. 58th Street, Forest Chase. opens at ten in the morning.
The breath of the digeridoo. Market Street No. 6. Starts at 10:30

Beach Styles

Nothing says "Aussie" quite like tanned skin, a freshly used surfboard, and a bikini tan. What should you gift your girlfriends in Perth? One can never have too many bathing suits. Make sure you pick up the beachwear that is almost as well-known as the large waves when you visit Cottesloe Beach.

You'll stand out at whatever resort you visit once you return home since swimwear companies like Seafolly, Zimmermann Wear, and White Sand Australia are more stylish than American faves like Billabong and Oakley. Beachwear presents are fantastic keepsakes from Perth that are useful in addition to being amazing.

Vintage

Searching around the tourist stores in Perth for antiques is perhaps one of the more unusual things to do there. The easiest way to change that, even if Perth may not be well-known worldwide, is to just go at the enormous assortment of retro Perth mementos that are offered.

On a gloomy day or as the centerpiece of your vacation, the souvenir stores in Perth have enough to keep you entertained, from local music recordings and apparel to fishing gear and fantastic furniture discoveries. The major attraction of these thrift stores is the opportunity to interact closely with the products; the meticulously curated selections emphasize detail, so take your time looking over each item. Antiques should unquestionably be on your list of things to purchase in Perth.

Visit these souvenir stores in Perth to make your discoveries of wonderful items:

Guildford, 141 James St., Curio Warehouse. opens at ten thirty in the morning.
Vintage Bluebird. Cambridge Street, Wemberley, 288. opens at ten in the morning.
Effies Guildford Emporium. Guildford's James Street, 141. opens at ten thirty in the morning.
Record Fat Shan. 37 Barrack St. The Basement. opens at ten in the morning.

Wine
With a vast variety of excellent wines produced by the vineyards, Swan Valley is one of Perth's most popular tourist attractions. Bringing home a fine bottle of wine, whether it's a dark red or white, is a wonderful way to treat the neighbors, make an impression on the employer, or surprise a loved one. Thus, be sure to pack the pleasure for later and enjoy the full-day vineyard excursions as well.

Check out these vineyards, even if they're not on your trip itinerary:

Vine Ugly Ducklings. 11:00am 7790 W Swan Rd. Shiraz liqueur is the best buy.
The Vineyard of Tyler. Padbury Avenue 301. 11:00 a.m. Red Grenache 2014 is the best buy.

Black & Coward Vineyards Swan Valley. 9 a.m. at 448 Harmans Mill Road. Semillion Sauvignon Blanc is the best deal.

Quokka

Put aside koalas and kangaroos; there's a new Aussie favorite in town. This adorable little cuddle bug would make any animal lover shout with delight, so you really must bring one home. There doesn't appear to be any damage in a stuffed animal version of the quokka making its way from the toy shop to the arms of friends and family back home, even if this is by no means an endorsement to go get a real quokka before departing Oz.

When visiting Perth with children, a quokka is sure to become their new best friend. These little Wallabies are adorable and resemble a cross between a kangaroo and a mouse. Visit the Perth Zoo to see these cute animals, then make your way to the gift store to pick up one for the trip home. This soft plush animal is a terrific choice for a Perth gift, and it's available at most souvenir stores in the city.

WHERE TO EAT

LOCAL CUISINE

Perth is quickly rising to the top of Australia's gourmet attractions, despite not having the same level of establishment as Sydney or Melbourne. Restaurants may enjoy an abundance of fresh seafood due to its proximity to the Indian Ocean, in addition to classic Australian fare like lamb and cattle. Additionally, the country's biggest producer of wheat is Western Australia. Perth's best foods span from well-known items like sourdough bread to regional specialties like a kangaroo.

Rock lobster
The most well-known seafood in Western Australia is the Western rock lobster, also referred to as crayfish. You can get fresh rock lobster off the boat at Cervantes, a two-hour drive north of Perth, but it's also available in the city.

For fresh local lobster, try the lobster at The Cray in Belmont or Joe's Fish Shack in the Fremantle fishing boat dock. Rock lobster is expensive in Western Australia, as it is in most other parts of the globe. A whole lobster in a restaurant will cost you at least $40.

Meatpie
Meat pies are quintessential Australian fare, and Perth produces some particularly excellent interpretations of this classic meal. You may experiment with tastes like mushrooms, poultry, mashed potato, or even cheese and bacon after you've had the

traditional beef and pastry version. We suggest Mary Street Bakery in Highgate or Tuck Shop café in Northbridge for a gourmet pie.

Pasta

Fremantle, Australia's westernmost port, used to be the first point of call for European immigrants traveling to Australia. Thousands of Italian immigrants settled in Perth during World War II, bringing with them the skills necessary to start a regional pasta craze.

Purists of fresh pasta will be pleased with Lulu La Delizia in Subiaco. The six-course seasonal tasting menu at Lalla Rookh is a must-try, and Garum is renowned for pairing excellent local meats with delicious pasta prepared in the Roman way.

Barramundi Indigenous to Australia and the Indo-Pacific region, barramundi is often referred to as Asian seabass. Even the most anti-seafood customers like the mild taste and minimal fat content of the white flesh. It's often served grilled in Perth, with a lovely crispy skin.

Excellent local fillets may be found at Sweetlips Fish Bar (Scarborough and Melville), while W Churchill in the city center serves delicious crispy skin barramundi.

Sourdough bread

Perth has a remarkable array of artisan bakeries that maximise the use of regional wheat. The city has been completely taken over by the sourdough movement, and almost every café serves freshly baked bread with creative toppings.

While Chu Bakery in Highgate specializes in toast and sweet delights, Bread in Common in Fremantle serves up easy and excellent sandwiches, cheeses, and sharing plates. Subiaco's Sorganic is the place to go for baguettes and breakfast.

kangaroo
Australia has more kangaroos than humans, and if you visit Western Australia, you can see a few of them jumping about in the countryside. You can get kangaroo meat in a lot of stores and restaurants if you'd want to try one too. A common description of the meat is that it tastes like an extremely lean cut of beef.

Furthermore, kangaroo meat is inexpensive, high in protein, and healthful. Sample some 'roo at Elizabeth Quay's Balthazar restaurant or the Little Creatures Brewery in Fremantle, where they also serve barramundi fishcakes. While the cuisine at Wildflower changes seasonally, kangaroo and other local fare are often offered.

TOP RESTAURANTS IN PERTH

Wildflower
Where: 1 Cathedral Ave, Perth
Perched atop the COMO The Treasury building, Wildflower offers a fine dining experience inspired by the Indigenous ethos of six seasons. With sweeping views of the city and a seasonal menu showcasing Western Australia's finest produce, this restaurant is perfect for those seeking an upscale, farm-to-table experience. Each dish reflects the richness of the land, featuring ingredients like native herbs and foraged flora. Paired with exceptional wines, Wildflower delivers a unique culinary journey that highlights local sustainability and creativity.

Long Chim
Where: State Buildings, 1 Cathedral Ave, Perth
Bringing the streets of Bangkok to Perth, Long Chim is a lively restaurant offering bold, authentic Thai flavors. Chef David Thompson, a master of Thai cuisine, has curated a menu full of fiery curries, fragrant stir-fries, and street-food-inspired snacks. The restaurant's casual yet energetic ambiance complements the vibrancy of the food. A must-try is the "Pad Thai" and the infamous "Chiang Mai Larp." For spice lovers, Long Chim delivers an unforgettable dining experience right in the heart of Perth.

Santini Bar & Grill
Where: 133 Murray Street, Perth
Located inside QT Perth, Santini Bar & Grill offers a blend of modern Italian cuisine with a focus on Mediterranean flavors. The stylish and energetic atmosphere is perfect for those seeking a social dining experience. Featuring wood-fired meats, house-

made pasta, and fresh seafood, Santini's dishes are crafted with locally sourced ingredients. The extensive wine list, featuring a mix of Australian and Italian selections, further enhances the dining experience, making it a popular choice for special occasions or a casual night out.

Bread in Common
Where: 43 Pakenham Street, Fremantle
Housed in a rustic, industrial building, Bread in Common is renowned for its hearty, wholesome dishes, many of which center around the restaurant's specialty: house-made bread. The menu focuses on shared plates, from wood-fired meats to fresh, vibrant salads, all made using locally sourced produce. The open kitchen and warm ambiance make for a relaxed yet lively dining experience. It's a favorite among locals for a casual brunch or a memorable dinner.

The Shorehouse
Where: 278 Marine Parade, Swanbourne
Set against the backdrop of the Indian Ocean, The Shorehouse is one of Perth's most picturesque dining spots. With a focus on relaxed coastal cuisine, the menu features an array of fresh seafood dishes, alongside light, summery fare like salads and grilled meats. Popular dishes include the chargrilled octopus and the yellowfin tuna crudo. The restaurant's vibrant atmosphere is enhanced by its spacious outdoor terrace, making it the ideal location for a long, leisurely lunch or sunset dinner.

Petition Kitchen

Where: State Buildings, St Georges Terrace, Perth
Petition Kitchen is a modern Australian restaurant that emphasizes a "from paddock to plate" philosophy. Located in the historic State Buildings, the restaurant offers a welcoming space with an open kitchen, where seasonal ingredients take center stage. From small share plates to more substantial meals, the menu reflects the diversity of Australian produce. Popular dishes include roast lamb with mint and grilled kangaroo. With a focus on sustainability, Petition Kitchen provides a fresh, modern take on classic Australian fare.

Il Lido Italian Canteen
Where: 88 Marine Parade, Cottesloe
Situated just steps from the beach, Il Lido Italian Canteen is the perfect spot for a relaxed yet sophisticated Italian dining experience. Known for its fresh pasta, delicious risotto, and seafood, Il Lido offers a menu filled with authentic Italian flavors made from locally sourced ingredients. The bustling, casual atmosphere is enhanced by friendly service and a vast wine list, making it an ideal location for both a quick meal and a long, leisurely dining experience by the ocean.

Manuka Woodfire Kitchen
Where: 134 High St, Fremantle
Manuka Woodfire Kitchen delivers a unique, rustic dining experience with its wood-fired cooking method at the core of its menu. The restaurant specializes in using sustainably sourced local produce, creating earthy, flavorful dishes in an intimate, cozy setting. Menu highlights include wood-fired seafood, slow-cooked

lamb, and vegetable dishes that emphasize simplicity and freshness. Paired with a thoughtful selection of wines, this is the place for a hearty, authentic meal that celebrates the flavors of Western Australia.

BEST CAFES AND BRUNCH SPOTS

1. Mary Street Bakery
Located in Highgate and several other spots across Perth, Mary Street Bakery is an institution in the city. Renowned for its freshly baked goods, artisan bread, and excellent coffee, it offers a laid-back atmosphere with a trendy edge. The café is famous for its doughnuts, but the brunch menu also boasts items like their signature fried chicken pancakes, house-made granola, and scrambled eggs with avocado on toast. Don't forget to try one of their homemade pastries before you leave.

2. Hylin
Hylin, located in West Leederville, offers a relaxed yet chic vibe, perfect for a weekend brunch with friends. Its menu is a delightful mix of simple but flavorful dishes, featuring avocado toast, bacon and egg rolls, and nourishing bowls filled with superfoods. Coffee enthusiasts will appreciate Hylin's focus on quality brews, made from beans sourced from local roasters. Their shaded outdoor area provides a cozy space to enjoy Perth's sunny mornings.

3. Tiisch
For those in search of a brunch with a bit of sophistication, Tiisch is the place to be. Situated in the heart of the city, this café serves an all-day brunch menu that's ideal for those who prefer to dine at a slower pace. The café's farm-to-table ethos shines through in

dishes like the smashed avocado on sourdough, eggs benedict, and the crowd-favourite shakshuka. With its minimalist décor and bright, airy space, Tiisch is both stylish and welcoming.

4. Gordon Street Garage

A former garage-turned café, Gordon Street Garage in West Perth is a popular spot for brunch-goers. With its industrial-chic interior and cozy vibe, it's the perfect place to settle in for a lazy morning. The menu is full of hearty, modern Australian dishes like corn fritters, poached eggs with dukkah, and smoked salmon bagels. The coffee here is exceptional, and their in-house roasting ensures that every cup is brewed to perfection.

5. Sayers Sister

Nestled in Northbridge, Sayers Sister offers a warm and inviting space with rustic décor and plenty of charm. The café is known for its inventive brunch menu, which includes dishes like brioche French toast, mushrooms on toast with poached eggs, and quinoa porridge with coconut and fresh berries. Their coffee is just as noteworthy, with a smooth and rich flavor that pairs perfectly with the freshly baked cakes and pastries on display.

6. Little Bird Café

For those seeking a health-conscious brunch, Little Bird Café in Northbridge is a great option. This bright and friendly café specializes in organic and gluten-free dishes, offering wholesome yet indulgent options. Their menu features items like acai bowls, smashed pumpkin on sourdough, and a vegan-friendly big breakfast. Little Bird also boasts a range of freshly squeezed juices, smoothies, and great coffee options for those looking to refresh and recharge.

7. Le Rebelle

This small, French-inspired bistro in Mount Lawley offers a unique brunch experience with a European twist. Le Rebelle is well known for its classic and refined dishes such as duck liver parfait, steak tartare, and croissants that are both flaky and buttery. While their dinner menu is also popular, brunch at Le Rebelle is a must-try for anyone looking for a more decadent and luxurious start to the day.

8. Chinta

For something a little different, Chinta in North Perth offers a unique tropical vibe with its Balinese-inspired setting. The café is famous for its vibrant décor, including hanging plants and lanterns, creating an exotic, tranquil atmosphere. The brunch menu at Chinta is equally exciting, with options like nasi goreng, coconut pancakes, and vegan bowls. It's the perfect spot for a relaxing brunch with a touch of escapism.

9. La Veen Coffee

La Veen Coffee is a popular café in the Perth CBD, known for its specialty coffee and minimalist design. The café sources its beans from some of the best local and international roasters, ensuring a superb cup of coffee every time. Their brunch offerings are simple but delicious, with avocado toast, ricotta hotcakes, and poached eggs with prosciutto being standouts. La Veen is the ideal spot for coffee lovers who also appreciate a well-executed brunch.

10. The Little Concept

This cozy café in Fremantle is a favorite among locals for its laid-back atmosphere and high-quality coffee. The Little Concept offers a great selection of vegan and vegetarian options, making it a go-to spot for those seeking plant-based meals. Their smashed avocado toast and smoothie bowls are particularly popular, along with their range of freshly baked goods. It's a charming spot to enjoy a relaxed morning away from the hustle and bustle.

WHERE TO STAY IN PERTH

LUXURY HOTELS AND RESORTS

1. COMO The Treasury

Located in the heart of Perth's historic district, COMO The Treasury is a luxurious five-star hotel that occupies beautifully restored heritage buildings. The hotel offers 48 spacious rooms and suites with contemporary interiors that exude elegance and comfort. Guests can enjoy access to world-class amenities, including a wellness spa, a state-of-the-art gym, and two acclaimed restaurants, Wildflower and Post. Prices start at around AUD 700 per night for a deluxe room, making it one of the most exclusive stays in Perth. Its central location provides easy access to the city's key attractions, including Elizabeth Quay and Kings Park.

2. Crown Towers Perth

Crown Towers is an iconic luxury resort located on the banks of the Swan River in Burswood, just minutes from Perth's CBD. With 500 stylish rooms and suites, this opulent hotel offers some of the finest accommodations in the city. Rooms boast floor-to-ceiling windows with stunning views of the river or city skyline. Crown Towers features a wide range of exclusive amenities, including a large outdoor pool, a premium spa, fine dining restaurants, and a vibrant casino. Prices start at around AUD 600 per night. The resort is ideal for those seeking a lavish experience with entertainment options at their fingertips.

3. The Ritz-Carlton, Perth

Perched on the Elizabeth Quay waterfront, The Ritz-Carlton, Perth offers unparalleled luxury with its sophisticated design and breathtaking views of the Swan River and the city skyline. The hotel has 205 well-appointed rooms and suites that combine modern elegance with local influences. Guests can indulge in the on-site spa, rooftop infinity pool, and fine dining at Hearth restaurant, which showcases local Western Australian produce. With rooms starting at approximately AUD 800 per night, The Ritz-Carlton is a top choice for travelers seeking a blend of luxury and natural beauty in Perth's vibrant city center.

4. InterContinental Perth City Centre

Located in the heart of Perth's bustling CBD, the InterContinental Perth City Centre combines modern luxury with timeless elegance. The hotel offers 240 chic rooms and suites featuring contemporary decor, plush bedding, and city views. Guests can enjoy dining at the hotel's Ascua restaurant, which serves Mediterranean-inspired cuisine, or relax at The Loft Lounge. Other amenities include a fitness center, business facilities, and personalized concierge services. Rooms at the InterContinental start from AUD 450 per night, making it a great option for both business and leisure travelers who want to stay in the city center without compromising on luxury.

5. Hyatt Regency Perth

Situated along the picturesque Swan River, the Hyatt Regency Perth is known for its sophisticated ambiance and world-class service. The hotel offers 367 rooms and suites, all featuring elegant furnishings, river or city views, and modern amenities. Guests can unwind by the outdoor pool, dine at the award-winning Café restaurant, or enjoy a drink at the Plain Street Bar.

The Hyatt Regency offers a balance of relaxation and accessibility, with rooms starting at around AUD 350 per night. Its location is ideal for visitors wanting to explore the city's cultural precincts while enjoying serene riverfront views.

BUDGET-FRIENDLY ACCOMMODATIONS

Budget

1. The Witch's Hat Backpackers Hostel

Located in the vibrant Northbridge area, The Witch's Hat is one of Perth's most popular budget hostels, known for its friendly atmosphere and convenient location. Just a short walk from the city center, this hostel offers both dormitory-style and private rooms at affordable rates, starting from AUD 30 per night for dorms and AUD 80 for private rooms. The hostel provides free Wi-Fi, a communal kitchen, a guest lounge, and an outdoor courtyard, making it a great place for socializing with fellow travelers. With its proximity to bars, restaurants, and public transport, it's a top choice for budget-conscious backpackers.

2. Billabong Backpackers Resort

Billabong Backpackers Resort offers a mix of dormitory and private rooms, starting from AUD 32 per night, located just minutes from the bustling Beaufort Street and Perth CBD. This resort-style hostel has a pool, an outdoor terrace, and a gym, giving guests access to amenities you wouldn't typically find in budget accommodations. The hostel also offers free breakfast, free Wi-Fi, and weekly social events, making it a fantastic option for budget travelers who want a little extra comfort. The hostel's laid-back vibe, combined with its proximity to shops, cafes, and nightlife, makes it ideal for young travelers.

3. City Perth Backpackers Hostel

Located in the heart of Perth, the City Perth Backpackers Hostel is an affordable and clean option for budget travelers. It offers dormitory rooms starting from AUD 28 per night and private rooms from AUD 80. The hostel provides free Wi-Fi, a communal kitchen, a lounge area, and laundry facilities. Its central location means you'll be within walking distance of the city's top attractions, including Kings Park, Elizabeth Quay, and the Perth Cultural Centre. For budget travelers looking for a simple, no-frills option with excellent access to the city, City Perth Backpackers is a great pick.

4. Britannia on William

Britannia on William is another affordable hostel in the heart of Northbridge, Perth's entertainment district. Dormitory rooms start at AUD 25 per night, and private rooms are available from AUD 70. The hostel features a communal kitchen, lounge, games room, and an outdoor courtyard, providing plenty of opportunities to relax and meet other travelers. It's just a short walk from Perth's main train station and popular attractions like the Art Gallery of Western Australia. Britannia on William is known for its laid-back, sociable environment, making it an excellent choice for those wanting to stay in a lively area at a budget price.

5. Ibis Budget Perth Airport

For those seeking budget accommodation close to Perth Airport, Ibis Budget Perth Airport offers a convenient and affordable option. Rooms start from AUD 100 per night, and while basic, they include comfortable beds, air conditioning, free Wi-Fi, and ensuite bathrooms. The hotel is ideal for travelers with early flights or short stays in Perth. It is located just 10 minutes from Perth Airport and offers easy access to public transportation into the city. Although the hotel lacks some of the amenities of more central options, its proximity to the airport and value for money make it a smart choice for travelers in transit.

FAMILY-FRIENDLY PLACES TO STAY

1. Parmelia Hilton Perth

Located in the heart of the city, Parmelia Hilton Perth is an excellent choice for families looking for a central location with luxurious amenities. The hotel offers spacious family rooms and interconnecting suites, with rates starting from AUD 250 per night. Families can enjoy the outdoor pool, fitness center, and on-site dining at the hotel's restaurant, which offers a kid-friendly menu. Parmelia Hilton is close to major attractions like Kings Park, Elizabeth Quay, and Perth Zoo, making it ideal for sightseeing. Babysitting services are also available upon request, allowing parents some time to unwind.

2. Fraser Suites Perth

Fraser Suites Perth offers a modern and spacious stay ideal for families. Located along the banks of the Swan River, this serviced apartment hotel provides one- and two-bedroom suites, perfect for families needing extra space. Rates start from AUD 200 per night. Each suite includes a fully equipped kitchen, living and dining areas, and laundry facilities, making it convenient for longer stays. The hotel also features an indoor heated pool and a fitness center. Its proximity to the Perth Mint and easy access to public transport make it a popular choice for families looking to explore the city.

3. Rendezvous Hotel Perth Scarborough

For families seeking a beachside retreat, the Rendezvous Hotel Perth Scarborough is an ideal choice. Located just steps from the beautiful Scarborough Beach, the hotel offers family rooms and ocean-view suites starting at AUD 180 per night. The hotel boasts a lagoon-style pool, kids' pool, and playground, ensuring plenty of entertainment for children. Families can also take advantage of the nearby beach activities, cafes, and walking paths along the coast. With its relaxed beach atmosphere and family-friendly amenities, Rendezvous is perfect for those looking for a mix of city and beach experiences.

4. The Sebel West Perth

The Sebel West Perth is an excellent option for families who prefer apartment-style accommodations with hotel services. Located in West Perth, this property offers studio and one-bedroom apartments, with rates starting from AUD 180 per night. Each apartment comes equipped with a kitchenette, free Wi-Fi, and a private balcony, giving families the flexibility to prepare their meals or relax after a day of exploring. The outdoor swimming pool and BBQ area are great for family gatherings, and the hotel's central location provides easy access to Kings Park and Perth's main attractions.

5. Crown Metropol Perth

Situated within the Crown Perth entertainment complex in Burswood, Crown Metropol Perth is a family favorite with its resort-style amenities. The hotel offers spacious family rooms and interconnecting suites, with prices starting from AUD 300 per night. One of the highlights is the large outdoor pool area, which includes a kids' splash zone, waterslides, and cabanas. Families can also enjoy a wide range of dining options within the complex, including restaurants that cater to children. With the casino, movie theaters, and riverside parklands nearby, Crown Metropol provides both entertainment and relaxation for families.

NIGHTLIFE AND ENTERTAINMENT

PERTH'S BEST BARS AND PUBS

1. Mechanics Institute

Nestled in Northbridge, the Mechanics Institute is one of Perth's most beloved small bars. Known for its laid-back vibe and rooftop setting, this hidden gem offers a wide selection of craft beers, creative cocktails, and an impressive range of whiskeys. The rooftop bar is the perfect spot for catching up with friends while enjoying views of the city skyline. Pair your drinks with a burger from the neighboring Flipside Burgers, which you can order directly from the bar. Drinks start from around AUD 10, making it a great spot for a casual night out.

2. The Aviary

Located in the heart of the Perth CBD, The Aviary is a stylish rooftop bar that boasts stunning views of the city. Its chic, open-air space is a hit with both locals and visitors, offering a vibrant atmosphere for afternoon drinks or evening cocktails. The menu features an extensive range of local and international beers, wines, and inventive cocktails, with prices starting from AUD 12. The Aviary also offers tasty bar bites and a lively ambiance, making it a perfect spot to enjoy Perth's warm weather while sipping on a refreshing drink.

3. The Bird

For those looking for a more eclectic and artsy vibe, The Bird in Northbridge is a great choice. This bar is known for its live music performances and creative events, offering everything from jazz to indie bands. The Bird is a small but intimate venue, attracting a cool crowd of music lovers and creatives. While the bar serves a variety of local beers and unique cocktails, it's the venue's cozy atmosphere and vibrant events that keep people coming back. Drinks are reasonably priced, with most options starting around AUD 8.

4. The Stables Bar

Situated in a historic horse stable, The Stables Bar offers a unique blend of old-world charm and contemporary design. Located just off Hay Street, this two-story venue is perfect for after-work drinks or weekend gatherings. The menu offers a variety of local and international beers, wines, and expertly crafted cocktails, starting at AUD 10. With its rustic courtyard and cozy indoor seating, The Stables Bar is a versatile venue for any occasion. The food menu also offers a great selection of modern Australian dishes, making it a popular spot for both food and drinks.

5. Petition Beer Corner

Located in the iconic State Buildings, Petition Beer Corner is a haven for beer enthusiasts. With over 20 beers on tap and a constantly rotating selection of local and international brews, this venue is a must-visit for anyone who appreciates craft beer. The knowledgeable staff are always on hand to recommend a new brew or talk you through the tasting notes. Prices for drinks vary depending on the beer, but most start at around AUD 8. The relaxed, communal atmosphere makes Petition Beer Corner a great spot to enjoy a casual drink with friends.

6. Helvetica

For whiskey lovers, Helvetica in Perth's CBD is a hidden treasure. Tucked away in a laneway, this sophisticated bar offers an extensive collection of local and international whiskeys, alongside a variety of high-quality spirits and cocktails. Whether you're a whiskey connoisseur or just getting started, the staff at Helvetica are known for their expertise and can guide you through their impressive menu. Whiskey flights and tasting sessions are available for those looking to expand their palate. Prices start from AUD 10 for standard drinks, but whiskey lovers may splurge on rare selections.

7. The Lucky Shag Waterfront Bar

Situated along the Swan River, The Lucky Shag Waterfront Bar offers a relaxed, casual atmosphere with spectacular river views. It's a great spot for afternoon drinks or a laid-back evening with friends. The bar offers a good selection of beers, wines, and cocktails, with prices starting at AUD 9. On weekends, live music and DJs add to the lively atmosphere, making it a favorite among locals and tourists alike. With its stunning location and casual vibe, The Lucky Shag is an excellent choice for a breezy outdoor drinking experience.

8. The Rosemount Hotel

A North Perth institution, The Rosemount Hotel is a favorite for both live music and a good pub experience. Known for hosting a wide range of live acts, from local bands to international performers, this venue has a great energy for music lovers. The spacious beer garden is perfect for a sunny afternoon, and the inside bar offers a more intimate setting. The drinks menu is varied, with craft beers, ciders, wines, and classic pub cocktails starting from AUD 9. The Rosemount is the go-to place for a quintessential pub experience combined with live entertainment.

LIVE MUSIC VENUES

Perth is a thriving cultural hub, with live music venues scattered across the city offering a diverse range of genres and atmospheres. From intimate bars to grand theatres, Perth caters to all kinds of music lovers.

1. The Astor Theatre

The Astor Theatre, located in Mount Lawley, is an iconic Art Deco building that dates back to the 1930s. This historic venue has hosted some of the best local and international artists across all genres. Its vintage charm and impressive acoustics make it a popular choice for concerts and live performances. The intimate seating arrangement offers a close-up view of the stage, and the atmosphere is electric, ensuring a memorable experience for concert-goers.

2. The Rosemount Hotel

One of Perth's most beloved live music venues, The Rosemount Hotel is renowned for its buzzing atmosphere and eclectic music lineup. Located in North Perth, the venue regularly showcases local talent and international acts across rock, indie, and alternative genres. The large beer garden also adds to its appeal, making it a favorite among those who enjoy an outdoor music experience.

3. Badlands Bar

Badlands Bar is a hidden gem for live music lovers in Perth. Known for its edgy vibe and underground atmosphere, this venue primarily features rock, punk, and heavy metal bands. The intimate space creates a raw and unfiltered experience for fans, making it a standout destination for discovering new and up-and-coming acts. With live music most nights of the week, Badlands Bar is a must-visit for those who enjoy the more rebellious side of the music scene.

4. The Ellington Jazz Club
For lovers of jazz, blues, and soul, The Ellington Jazz Club is Perth's go-to venue. Situated in Northbridge, this stylish and intimate venue offers live jazz performances almost every night. The club's cozy atmosphere, combined with high-quality performances from both local and international musicians, provides a unique and sophisticated musical experience. The Ellington also hosts regular jam sessions and late-night performances, keeping the music alive into the early hours.

5. Mojos Bar
Located in Fremantle, Mojos Bar is another intimate venue that has earned its reputation as a staple of Perth's live music scene. Specializing in indie, rock, and alternative music, Mojos Bar is a hub for discovering new talent. With a laid-back, quirky vibe and a strong focus on promoting local musicians, it's the perfect spot for those seeking a more relaxed live music experience.

THEATRE AND PERFORMING ARTS

Perth also has a flourishing theatre and performing arts scene, with venues that cater to everything from drama and opera to ballet and contemporary dance.

1. His Majesty's Theatre

An iconic landmark in the heart of Perth, His Majesty's Theatre is one of Australia's finest examples of Edwardian architecture. Built-in 1904, it is a grand venue with a capacity of over 1,200 seats. The theatre hosts an array of performances, from opera and ballet to plays and musicals. Its stunning interior and historical significance make attending a performance here a truly special experience. His Majesty's Theatre is also home to the West Australian Opera and West Australian Ballet, providing a platform for world-class productions year-round.

2. State Theatre Centre of Western Australia

Located in Northbridge, the State Theatre Centre is one of Perth's premier performing arts venues. With multiple performance spaces, including the 575-seat Heath Ledger Theatre, it offers a diverse range of productions from classical theatre and contemporary dance to experimental and avant-garde performances. The venue's modern architecture and state-of-the-art facilities make it a top choice for both local and international theatre companies.

3. Perth Concert Hall

Perth Concert Hall is renowned for its exceptional acoustics and is considered one of the best venues in Australia for orchestral and classical performances. Home to the West Australian Symphony Orchestra (WASO), the concert hall also hosts a variety of other events, including contemporary music concerts, recitals, and stand-up comedy. The elegant design and riverside location provide a scenic backdrop for some of the city's finest performances.

4. The Blue Room Theatre

A smaller yet influential venue, The Blue Room Theatre is located in Northbridge and is known for supporting independent and emerging artists. This intimate space focuses on experimental and innovative productions, giving voice to new talent in Perth's theatre scene. The venue's atmosphere is intimate and engaging, offering audiences a chance to see bold and original performances up close.

5. Regal Theatre

Situated in Subiaco, the Regal Theatre is another historic venue that has played a central role in Perth's performing arts culture. With its Art Deco design and seating for over 1,000 guests, the Regal Theatre hosts a wide range of performances, from plays and musicals to comedy shows and concerts. Its grand design and vintage charm create a nostalgic experience for audiences while enjoying modern productions.

TRAVEL TIPS AND SAFETY

STAYING SAFE IN PERTH

Perth is a relatively safe city for travelers, but like any other major urban area, it's important to be cautious and stay aware of your surroundings.

1. General Safety
Crime Rates: Perth has a low crime rate, but petty crimes like pickpocketing and bag snatching can occur, especially in tourist-heavy areas. Keep your belongings close, particularly in crowded places, and avoid flashing valuable items such as jewelry or electronics.

Public Transport: The city's public transport system is generally safe, but it's a good idea to avoid isolated bus or train stations late at night. Stick to well-lit areas and opt for ride-share services or taxis when traveling late in the evening.

Beach Safety: Perth's beaches are stunning, but be mindful of ocean safety. Always swim between the flags at patrolled beaches, as these areas are monitored by lifeguards. Pay attention to any warnings about rip currents or dangerous marine life like jellyfish and sharks.

Sun Protection: The Australian sun can be harsh, especially in Perth's hot summer months. Wear sunscreen with a high SPF, a hat, and sunglasses, and stay hydrated by drinking plenty of water, particularly during outdoor activities.

2. Scams and Tourist Traps

While scams targeting tourists are not common in Perth, it's always good to be cautious when dealing with unsolicited offers or purchasing from unfamiliar vendors. Stick to official ticket counters and registered service providers for tours and activities.

3. Safe Areas

Most of Perth's central areas and suburbs are safe to explore, particularly during the day. Neighborhoods like Northbridge and Mount Lawley are popular for nightlife but can become rowdy after dark. Use common sense, travel with friends when possible, and avoid overly intoxicated crowds.

HEALTH AND EMERGENCY CONTACTS

1. Healthcare and Pharmacies

Healthcare: Australia has a high standard of healthcare, and there are many medical facilities available in Perth. If you're traveling from overseas, it's wise to have travel insurance that covers medical expenses, as healthcare costs for non-residents can be high.

Pharmacies: Pharmacies are widespread in Perth and offer a range of over-the-counter medications. Chemist Warehouse and Priceline are two major pharmacy chains where you can buy travel essentials, including sunscreen, first aid supplies, and any basic health needs.

2. Emergency Numbers

Emergency Services: The national emergency number in Australia is 000. This connects you to police, fire, or ambulance services. It's a good idea to keep this number handy throughout your trip.

Local Hospitals: For non-emergency health issues, Royal Perth Hospital and Fiona Stanley Hospital are major healthcare facilities that cater to visitors and locals alike. Many hospitals have emergency departments in case of urgent medical attention.

3. Travel Insurance

Having comprehensive travel insurance is highly recommended when visiting Perth, as it covers unexpected health issues, accidents, or travel disruptions. Ensure that your insurance includes medical evacuation in case you need to be transferred for treatment.

LOCAL ETIQUETTE AND CUSTOMS

1. Tipping

Tipping is not mandatory in Australia but is appreciated for good service. In restaurants and cafes, a tip of around 10% of the bill is common for excellent service. However, it's completely at your discretion and not expected. For taxis, rounding up the fare or adding a small tip is polite, but again, not obligatory.

2. Greetings and Social Etiquette

Australians are generally very friendly and laid-back. A simple "hello" or "g'day" is a common greeting. When meeting someone for the first time, a firm handshake and eye contact are standard. Australians value politeness, so saying "please" and "thank you" is expected in all interactions.

3. Environmental Awareness

Australia is known for its beautiful natural environment, and locals take conservation seriously. When visiting parks, beaches, or nature reserves, always clean up after yourself and use recycling bins where available. Water conservation is also important, so be mindful of your water use during your stay, especially in a city like Perth, which experiences long dry seasons.

4. Smoking

Smoking is banned in most indoor public spaces, including restaurants, bars, and public transport areas. There are also restrictions in outdoor dining spaces and near children's playgrounds. Look for designated smoking areas if you need to smoke.

5. Indigenous Culture

Australia has a rich Indigenous culture, and it's important to respect the traditions and history of the local Aboriginal people. In Perth, the Noongar people are the traditional custodians of the land. Some areas, such as sacred sites, may have restrictions on access. It's also considered respectful to ask for permission before taking photos of Indigenous art or cultural artifacts.

CONCLUSION

As your journey through Perth draws to a close, I hope this guide has been your trusted companion, shedding light on the wonders of this vibrant city. From the sun-kissed shores of Cottesloe Beach to the bustling energy of the city's cultural heart, Perth leaves an indelible mark on the soul of every traveler. The golden sunsets over the Indian Ocean, the endless blue skies, and the warm smiles of the locals are just some of the unforgettable moments you'll carry with you long after you've left.

Whether you marveled at the wildlife in Kings Park, felt the pulse of live music in the city's venues, or simply wandered through its quiet streets, Perth offers a unique blend of serenity and excitement. It's a city that embraces both the simplicity of nature and the creativity of urban life. Don't forget the practical tips that helped guide you: stay hydrated under the blazing sun, keep safety in mind while exploring, and always be open to learning the customs of the land.

I'm truly grateful that you've allowed me to be a part of your Perth adventure. Every turn you took, every hidden gem you discovered, added another layer of depth to this journey. But remember, this is just the beginning—Perth's beauty extends beyond its iconic landmarks. There's always something more to uncover, something new to experience.

I encourage you to keep exploring, to venture beyond the familiar, and to let curiosity guide your next adventure. Whether you're drawn back to Perth or off to another corner of the world, let the spirit of discovery stay with you. The world is wide, full of surprises, and always waiting for you to take that next step.

So, what's next on your horizon? Wherever you go, remember to embrace the moment, savor the experiences, and let your travels shape the stories of your life.

Safe travels,
Your fellow explore